OSPREY MILITARY

CA W9-BUN-730 6

BALACLAVA 1854

▼ *View from Balaclava. The view from the Marine Heights after the Battle of Balaclava, looking towards Sevastopol. The village of Kamara, which fell to General Gribbe at 6am on 25 October, is nestling beneath the peak on the extreme right. The whitish mound in the centre is Canrobert's Hill; the North Valley is the dark expanse beyond. The Causeway Heights run to the left of Canrobert's Hill, and the rugged ground over which the Heavy Brigade charged can thus be seen. Balaclava harbour is on the left. (Sandhurst)*

GENERAL EDITOR DAVID G. CHANDLER

OSPREY MILITARY

CAMPAIGN SERIES

6

BALACLAVA 1854

THE CHARGE OF
THE LIGHT BRIGADE

JOHN SWEETMAN

▼*Chersonese Uplands. The position on the right of the Allied line before Sevastopol occupied by the British 2nd Division. On the right is the Sapoune Ridge overlooking the Tchernaya valley. The left back-ground depicts the batteries and fortifications of Sevastopol. Troops here were almost seven miles from Balaclava, and the difficulty of bringing up supplies, even in good weather, is self-evident. (Sandhurst)*

Acknowledgements

I am grateful to the following for permission to reproduce photographic material: The Commandant, The Royal Military Academy Sandhurst; Mr. B. Mollo; Mr. J. M. Selby; Mr. P. A. Warner; and the David Paul Collection. My thanks are also due to Mr. R. B. Goodall for producing the first-class photographs used in this book.
                                                        J.S.

FOR A CATALOGUE OF ALL BOOKS PUBLISHED BY OSPREY MILITARY, AUTOMOTIVE AND AVIATION PLEASE WRITE TO:

The Marketing Manager, Osprey Direct USA, PO Box 130, Sterling Heights, MI 48311-0130, USA.
Email: info@ospreydirectusa.com

The Marketing Manager, Osprey Direct UK, PO Box 140, Wellingborough, Northants, NN8 4ZA, United Kingdom.
Email: info@ospreydirect.co.uk

VISIT OPSREY AT
www.ospreypublishing.com

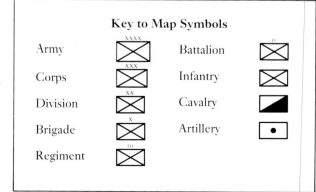

CONTENTS

First published in Great Britain in 1990 by Osprey Publishing, Elms Court, Chapel Way, Botley, Oxford OX2 9LP, United Kingdom.
Email: info@ospreypublishing.com

British Library Cataloguing in Publication Data
Sweetman, John, *1935–*
Balaclava 1854 and the charge of the Light Brigade. – (Osprey campaign series; v.6).
1. Crimean War
I. Title
947.073
ISBN 0-85045-961-3

Produced by DAG Publications Ltd for Osprey Publishing Ltd.
Colour bird's eye view illustrations by Cilla Eurich.
Cartography by Micromap.
Wargaming Balaclava by Arthur Harman.
Wargames consultant Duncan Macfarlane.
Typeset by Typesetters (Birmingham) Ltd, Warley.
Mono camerawork by M&E Reproductions, North Fambridge, Essex.
Printed in China through World Print Ltd.

PREPARATION: ADVANCE TO BALACLAVA

On 14 September 1854, troops of a British Expeditionary Force, led by Lord FitzRoy Raglan, began to land on the shores of the Crimean peninsula at Calamita Bay, 32 miles north of their ultimate objective, the Russian naval port of Sevastopol. Ahead lay eighteen months of unexpected misery for those lucky enough to survive. A short punitive campaign, culminating in swift seizure of Sevastopol, would prove just a pipe-dream.

Origins of the War

There were long-standing reasons for the war in which Raglan's army had become involved. Britain feared that Russia would overrun the declining Turkish Empire, which sprawled both sides of the Bosphorus Straits into Asia Minor and south-eastern Europe. Since the eighteenth century, successive tsars had expanded south into the Ukraine and Crimea, and further east into the Caucasus. They threatened to crush Turkey in a powerful vice. However, the Caucasus region, hilly and sparsely populated, presented formidable military problems.

The Balkans, in south-eastern Europe below the River Danube where it flows into the Black Sea, were a different proposition. The nationalities there were not Slavonic but were mostly Christian. Russia felt a particular affinity to them. Establishing a religious protectorship over Turkey's fourteen million Balkan subjects thus became a major aim of the Tsar. That this would allow a degree of political influence in Turkey was an undeniable bonus, for Russia harboured one burning ambition – control of the Bosphorus and Dardanelles, thus allowing passage of warships from Sevastopol (her main Black Sea base) into the Mediterranean. To achieve this, the Tsar must dominate Turkey and, ideally, gain ascendancy in Constantinople.

The prospect of such a development thoroughly alarmed the British government. Nor was the danger pure fantasy. During the Greek War of Independence (1821–9), a Russian army had invaded the Balkans, advancing to within reach of Constantinople. Only pressure from other European powers had secured its withdrawal. During a prolonged dispute (1831–41) between Turkey and the ruler of Egypt, Mehemet Ali (who was nominally the Sultan's vassal), Russia almost succeeded in gaining not only the religious influence that she sought in the Balkans but much wider power over the Turkish government politically in return for military assistance. Secretly, the Sultan agreed to close the Straits on Russian demand to all foreign warships. Learning about it, Britain took the lead in foiling this subterfuge.

Viewing Turkey as 'the sick man of Europe' – about to disintegrate and therefore ripe for picking – Tsar Nicholas I would not rest, however. A minor religious dispute gave him an opportunity to try again. A quarrel broke out in 1852 over guardianship of holy places in Jerusalem (then Turkish), and Russia once more pressed her claim for protectorship over the Balkan Christians. British warships had persuaded Russia not to undermine Turkey in the past, so in June 1853 a fleet under Vice-Admiral Dundas sailed from Malta to 'the neighbourhood of the Dardanelles . . . for the protection of Turkey against an unprovoked attack and in defence of her independence'. The Tsar was clearly unimpressed. Shortly afterwards, he sent troops across his south-western border to occupy Moldavia and Wallachia (modern Romania, then two provinces of Turkey) to obtain 'without war . . . her [Russia's] just demands'. He was, the Tsar claimed, going 'to the defence of the Orthodox religion'. Of that, neither Turkey nor other European powers were convinced.

A Turkish ultimatum to withdraw went unheeded, and on 23 October 1853 the Sultan at length declared war. The previous day, British and French warships had entered the Black Sea. Yet, at this stage, neither France nor Britain seriously considered an expeditionary force on land. Strong Turkish defences, considerably strengthened since Russia's last advance southwards more than twenty years before, barred the enemy's route along the Danube. In Britain there was neither the public enthusiasm nor the political will to get further embroiled. The Turks seemed in command of the situation. Dramatically, all of this changed with the 'massacre' of 4,000 Turkish sailors in Sinope

▲ *Nicholas I, Tsar of Russia. Grandson of Catherine the Great, who did much to expand Russian territory to the shores of the Black Sea, Nicholas was born in 1796 as Russia's hold over the Crimea was being consolidated. From an early age interested in military matters, he held a series of army appointments rising to the rank of lieutenant-general before becoming tsar in 1825. Once on the throne, he showed particular interest in Turkey, which he described as 'the sick man of Europe'. He was* confident that the Allies would be defeated, even after they had landed in the Crimea. Upset by the defeat on the Alma, he nevertheless would not think of abandoning Sevastopol. Nicholas prompted Menshikov to attack across the Tchernaya, which led directly to the Battle of Balaclava. Eventually depressed by lack of Russian success, Nicholas dismissed Menshikov from his command in February 1855, only a few days before his own death. (David Paul)

▲ *Vice-Admiral Sir James Dundas. Commander of the British fleet which was ordered first to 'the neighbourhood of the Dardanelles' as a warning to Russia that her military action in the Balkans was unacceptable, and then in conjunction with a French fleet entered the Black Sea in January 1854. He subsequently sent a squadron to bombard Odessa, when a British vessel was fired on while evacuating diplomatic staff. Dundas commanded the fleet quite independently of the land force commander (Lord* Raglan), and could only be asked for his help to support army operations. The fleet was ineffective against Sevastopol. Before the war ended, he was to be replaced in the Black Sea command by Sir Edmund Lyons. (David Paul)

harbour 300 miles east of Constantinople on 30 November 1853 by a Russian naval squadron firing explosive shells rather than solid round shot. In the press and in enthusiastic public meetings the British government was urged to act positively: by deploying their fleets alone, the British and French had interfered only 'to betray unfortunate Turkey'. Lord Aberdeen's ministers were portrayed as 'the imbecile men, the minions of Russia': and a *Punch* cartoon showed the Prime Minister blackening the Tsar's boots. *The Westminster Review* then touched a sensitive, commercial nerve, when it argued that 'our passage to India . . . [and] our commerce with all free nations' were at risk.

More mindful than an ill-informed public about the difficulties of becoming entangled in war with such a large and powerful enemy, the British and French governments moved cautiously. On 4 January 1854, their fleets entered the Black Sea with the incredible orders (considering that neither country was yet at war with Russia) to attack Russian warships if they refused to return to port. Demands for action against Nicholas I (portrayed as 'that fiend in human form') built up, as diplomatic hopes of solving the crisis dimmed. On 27 February, in a final attempt to convince the Tsar that Britain was indeed serious, the Foreign Secretary issued an ultimatum to St. Petersburg. An undertaking to withdraw from Moldavia and Wallachia by 30 April must be forthcoming within six days: 'Refusal or silence . . . [would be] equivalent to a declaration of war.' Nicholas I did not deign to react. So Britain entered what was then known as 'The War With Russia', but later became recognized as 'The Crimean War', for it was there that the bulk of the fighting was to occur.

On 27 March, Queen Victoria informed Parliament 'that Her Majesty feels bound to afford active assistance to her ally the Sultan against unprovoked aggression'. A formal treaty of alliance was signed with France on 10 April, to which Turkey acceded five days later. And military action was not thereafter long delayed. Already, on 11 March, Sir Charles Napier had sailed with a

▼ *Bombardment of Odessa. This sketch by an officer who took part in the action shows the Imperial Mole at Odessa being destroyed on 22 April 1854. British and French warships pounded Odessa, on the northern shore of the Black Sea, after the ship sent to evacuate the British and French consuls under a flag of truce on 13 April had been fired on by shore batteries. Three days later, seventeen British warships discharged a 900-gun broadside to signal a punitive operation that would continue intermittently for another six days. This explosion was shortly followed by a truce. (David Paul)*

▲ FitzRoy James Henry Somerset, Baron Raglan. Eleventh child of the Duke of Beaufort, FitzRoy Somerset served as the Duke of Wellington's Military Secretary during the Peninsular War and at Waterloo, where he lost an arm. From 1818 until 1852, FitzRoy Somerset served in senior administrative appointments either in support of the Master-General of the Ordnance or the Commander-in-Chief of the Army in London. During these years, he did not see active service. In 1852 created Baron Raglan, he became Master-General of the Ordnance before being appointed to command the Expeditionary Force to the East in February 1852. Promoted general (June 1854) and field marshal (December 1854), he was to die in the Crimea in June 1855. (Selby)

▲ Lieutenant-General Sir George Brown. A firm believer in discipline, as a young officer he had fought with Sir John Moore in the Peninsula. Brown had held a number of senior staff appointments (including adjutant-general at the Horse Guards) since 1815. Although the senior divisional commander, Brown was not given a 'dormant commission' to succeed Raglan if he were ill or incapacitated during the campaign. That went to Sir George Cathcart. But, in Bulgaria, when Raglan received orders to invade the Crimea and capture Sevastopol, he turned to Brown for advice. As commander of the Light Division, Brown would not be directly involved at Balaclava. (David Paul)

fleet from Portsmouth for the Baltic under the watchful eye of the Queen in the royal yacht *Fairy*. In the Black Sea, enraged at shore batteries opening fire while diplomatic talks were taking place under a flag of truce, seventeen warships pounded Odessa with their broadsides. Sevastopol also came under attack, as the mouth of the Danube was blockaded, and the shores of the Sea of Azov and the Caucasus were reconnoitred.

The Expeditionary Force Musters

In England, from early 1854 as the political situation deteriorated, an Expeditionary Force – originally simply designated 'for the East' – had been gradually assembling. Lord Raglan, a sixty-four year old Peninsula veteran, the Duke of Wellington's former Military Secretary and currently Master-General of the Ordnance, would be its commander. Undoubtedly brave (first into the breach at Badajoz, and losing an arm at Waterloo), Raglan had never commanded troops in battle, however; and for most of the past forty years he had held purely administrative posts. His divisional commanders also had varied experience: just one was under sixty, and only two had led a division in battle.

The Queen's 35-year-old cousin, the Duke of Cambridge, who had never been in action before, was chosen to lead the 1st Division. The 2nd was put in more experienced hands: Sir George de Lacy Evans (aged 67) had served in the Peninsula, India and during the Carlist Wars of the 1830s in Spain. His subsequent career had been blighted to some extent by his radical politics and a suspicion of certain disloyalty towards superior officers. The 3rd Division's commander, Sir Richard England (aged 61), had less experience than de Lacy Evans, although he had served in India and during the

▲ Major-General The Earl of Lucan. George Charles Bingham, Earl of Lucan, had commanded the 17th Lancers (1826–37), showing himself to be obsessed not only with discipline but with finery. Under his control, the regiment drilled constantly and worked hard: punishments for minor breaches of discipline were strictly applied, with floggings commonplace. Critics referred to his 'martinet zeal . . . lack of self-control and unpopularity' with his officers. Using his own money, he set out to make the 17th Lancers a well turned out regiment, so that they became known as 'Bingham's Dandies'. Given command of the Cavalry Division in the Crimea, he was to some extent unlucky to have his brother-in-law, Lord Cardigan, in command of the Light Brigade. The men detested each other. (Selby)

▲ Lieutenant-General His Royal Highness The Duke of Cambridge. Thirty-five year old cousin of Queen Victoria, George William Frederick Charles, Duke of Cambridge, commanded the 1st Infantry Division in the Crimea. Having previously served in the Hanoverian Army, he briefly commanded the 17th Lancers during the Chartist troubles in England, then held administrative appointments in Corfu and Ireland. He led the 1st Division at the Battle of the Alma and played a small part in the closing stages of the Battle of Balaclava, though not until its four main phases were over. After the war he was to become Commander-in-Chief of the Army from 1856 to 1895. (David Paul)

Kaffir Wars in southern Africa. Sixty-year-old Sir George Cathcart led the 4th Division; with previous service in colonial campaigns, Cathcart held a 'dormant commission', which provided for him to take over if Raglan were incapacitated. Sir George Brown, like Raglan aged 64, took charge of the fifth infantry division, the Light Division. A strict disciplinarian, Brown had fought with distinction in the Peninsula and since 1815 had held a succession of influential staff appointments.

Of the five commanders of infantry divisions, only the Duke of Cambridge and Cathcart would be marginally involved in the Battle of Balaclava. The onus of that day would fall on the Cavalry Division. Its commander, Lord Lucan (aged 54) was a military martinet, somewhat similar in this respect to Sir George Brown. A former commanding officer of the 17th Lancers (who would ride with the Light Brigade at Balaclava) and in his early years briefly attached to the Russian staff on

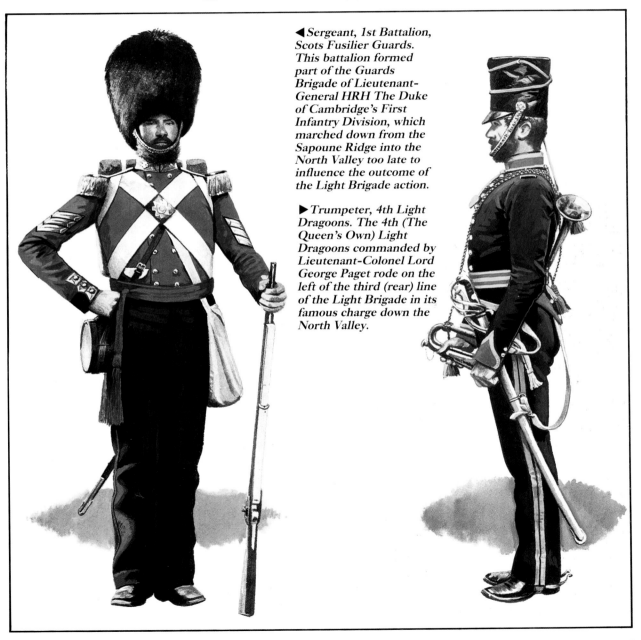

◀ Sergeant, 1st Battalion, Scots Fusilier Guards. This battalion formed part of the Guards Brigade of Lieutenant-General HRH The Duke of Cambridge's First Infantry Division, which marched down from the Sapoune Ridge into the North Valley too late to influence the outcome of the Light Brigade action.

▶ Trumpeter, 4th Light Dragoons. The 4th (The Queen's Own) Light Dragoons commanded by Lieutenant-Colonel Lord George Paget rode on the left of the third (rear) line of the Light Brigade in its famous charge down the North Valley.

◀ Lieutenant-General Sir John Fox Burgoyne. Illegitimate son of the general who surrendered to the American colonists at Saratoga (1777), Sir John was already 71 when sent to Constantinople with Colonel Ardent, a French engineer, to survey the Turkish defences in advance of the Expeditionary Force. A very experienced engineer, he had served throughout the Peninsular War and subsequently been chairman of the Public Works Board in Ireland (1831–45). Once the Allies landed in the Crimea, he remained attached to Lord Raglan's staff and was particularly influential in advising on the 'flank march' round Sevastopol to Balaclava and the conduct of the siege operations from the Chersonese Uplands. (Selby)

▼Departure of the Grenadier Guards. This contemporary print depicts the Grenadier Guards marching through Trafalgar Square on 22 February 1854 on their way to Waterloo Station. The scene is typical of many such departures: men cheering, children running alongside the troops, women looking pensive. Note the colours and mounted officers in the background. (David Paul)

campaign, Lucan heartily detested his 57-year-old brother-in-law, Lord Cardigan, who, by an unfortunate twist of fate, secured command of the Light Brigade in the Crimea. The Heavy Brigade went to the Hon. James Scarlett, aged 55 and, like Cardigan, without active service experience.

Lord Raglan had considerable influence over the choice of his senior commanders and his immediate staff officers (the Expeditionary Force's military secretary, quartermaster-general, adjutant-general as well as his personal aides-de-camp), but the regiments allocated to the divisions were determined by the administrative head of the Army at the Horse Guards in London, the Commander-in-Chief (Lord Hardinge). Hardinge controlled neither the artillery nor engineers, however; nominally, Raglan did that, as Master-General of the Ordnance. In 1854 his deputy (Lieutenant-General Sir Hew Ross) made the ordnance arrangements for the Expeditionary Force. En route, the Royal Navy would protect the troops, who were to be transported in a motley collection of sailing and steam vessels, many of which had been specially requisitioned. Once ashore, land transport and supplies (other than strictly military needs, such as ammunition) were provided (or not, as it turned out) by the Commissariat Department – a civilian organization answerable to the Treasury in London. To say the least, the commander of the Expeditionary Force faced a difficult task, quite apart from securing the defeat of the enemy. With no direct control over the Commissariat, having to request assistance (even direct cooperation in operations) from an independent admiral, who could always claim inability to act without express authority from the Admiralty 3,000 miles away, and aware that the Ordnance troops in theory (and often in practice) owed their ultimate allegiance to London, Raglan must also deal with the French and Turkish commanders on an equal footing. (In contrast, during the Peninsular War, Wellington had been in overall command of British, Portuguese and Spanish forces.) To make matters worse, at the time of Balaclava, the British had fewer troops in the Crimea than either of their allies.

All these problems lay in the future as, even before the British ultimatum expired, troops began to leave England for Turkey. Their precise role was not certain. Some no doubt hoped that they might only get as far as Malta before the Russians saw that the Allies were in earnest and backed down. At worst, the defence of Constantinople against a Russian advance through the Balkans was foreseen. So a 71-year-old, experienced engineer (Sir John Fox Burgoyne) was sent with a French officer to assess the strength of the Turkish defences.

To the Black Sea

On 22 February, the Grenadier and Coldstream Guards left Southampton for the Mediterranean, the first Expeditionary Force units to so do. Soon afterwards, the Second Battalion the Rifle Brigade cleared Portsmouth, and on 28 February the Scots Fusilier Guards paid tribute to the Royal Family at Buckingham Palace before marching on to Waterloo Station amid scenes of delirious excitement. Emotional crowds waved the trains away to the south coast. Throughout the next three months, transports sailed from a number of ports, stopping off at Gibraltar before reaching Malta. There, action seemed far off. The mild climate encouraged relaxation. Cheap local wine became popular; in the Union Club officers and wives (many of whom had travelled independently via France) danced many a night away.

It could not last. On 30 March troops began to leave for Turkey. Arriving at Gallipoli on 8 April, they found a distinct lack of accommodation and food. The French had beaten them to the best areas. By the end of May some 18,000 British and 22,000 French troops were crowded around this tiny town, condemned by the disillusioned as 'rickety, dirty and dilapadated [with] abominable collections of stagnant filth, reeking with unbearable odours'. To their relief, early in June, most of the British sailed north to Constantinople and Scutari – but there conditions were disappointingly no better, and extreme heat added to the troops' discomfort. Many took solace in alcohol: one night, 2,400 British drunks were reported.

Partly because the military situation along the Danube remained unresolved – the Russians still being threateningly massed in the two provinces –

◀Gibraltar. After battling their way across the Bay of Biscay, which was torn by seasonable storms, the troopships put in for a short stay at Gibraltar. Here the soldiers climbed the narrow Main Street to barter with Moors in their flowing robes, Spaniards and local Gibraltarians for goods from tobacco to soap and, inevitably, wine. Above, the guns of the fortress offered a silent menace to would-be attackers. (David Paul)

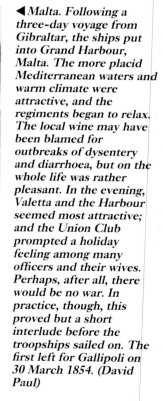

◀Malta. Following a three-day voyage from Gibraltar, the ships put into Grand Harbour, Malta. The more placid Mediterranean waters and warm climate were attractive, and the regiments began to relax. The local wine may have been blamed for outbreaks of dysentery and diarrhoea, but on the whole life was rather pleasant. In the evening, Valetta and the Harbour seemed most attractive; and the Union Club prompted a holiday feeling among many officers and their wives. Perhaps, after all, there would be no war. In practice, though, this proved but a short interlude before the troopships sailed on. The first left for Gallipoli on 30 March 1854. (David Paul)

◀Lord Raglan. A contemporary engraving, showing clearly the disability which the British Commander-in-Chief incurred at Waterloo. Determined to overcome the loss of his right arm quickly, very soon after the limb had been amputated, he wrote a note with his left hand. Once in Bulgaria, in July 1854, Raglan was ordered by the Secretary of State for War (the Duke of Newcastle) to attack the Crimea and take Sevastopol, unless he could put forward a good reason for not doing so. Lack of reliable information about the enemy's strength and dispositions might have been argued; but Raglan believed that he must do his duty. That is what his mentor, the Duke of Wellington, would have counselled. (David Paul)

and partly to seek out cooler quarters, after a brief stay many of the British and French sailed on into the Black Sea to Varna in Turkish-held Bulgaria. The first impression from the sea of a delightful little port was swiftly shattered on closer inspection. The streets were narrow, pot-holed and each angled towards a putrid central drain. And, once more, the French quickly established themselves in the best available accommodation. From the military standpoint, newly built piers proved inadequate for the size of the force seeking disembarkation: horses were loaded precariously into rowing boats to be carried kicking and squealing ashore. This was an unopposed landing in friendly territory. Lord Raglan already knew that he might have to invade the Crimea. The omens for that exercise, judging by the performance at Varna, were far from good.

Varna and its immediate hinterland obviously could not sustain an Allied force now of 50,000, so many British regiments moved some twenty miles inland to the valleys of Devna and Aladyn on the road to the Turkish headquarters at Shumla and, also, well placed to block Russian penetration south of the Danube. The attractive settings of the new camps soon proved false. Supplies of wild fruit and deer were quickly exhausted by eager foragers. Much more critically, mortal disease struck the lines. Cholera appeared in the French camps on 11 July and rapidly spread to the British;

▲ Constantinople. After a short stay at Gallipoli, owing to lack of accommodation or space to pitch tents in the area because too many British and French troops had concentrated there, many of the regiments moved north to Constantinople. Although attractive from the deck of a troopship, on closer inspection the Turkish capital seemed distinctly seedy. One disillusioned Briton wrote: 'Of all the villainous holes that I have ever been in, this is, I think the worst.' The culture shock for those unfamiliar with eastern habits and practices proved too great to accept. With some relief, the order to sail on to Bulgaria came after a short time. (Selby)

600 men died in a fortnight. Tents were hastily moved. But the fresh locations helped little. Then, on 10 August, a fire in Varna destroyed much-needed stores. Soon cholera spread to the fleets off-shore.

Amid this confusion and death, plans began in earnest to invade the Crimea. Incredibly, on 26 June the Russians had lifted the siege of the Turkish fortress of Silistra on the Danube and, by 2 August, had withdrawn completely from Moldavia and Wallachia. Yet political and public opinion in London and Paris would not let the troops come home without a fight. On 16 July, Raglan received a dispatch from the Cabinet: 'The fortress [Sevastopol] must be reduced and the fleet taken or destroyed: nothing but insuperable impediments . . . should be allowed to prevent the early decision to undertake these operations'.

▲Omar Pasha. The Turkish Commander-in-Chief held an independent command in the Crimea. Lord Raglan would have to consult with him and with the French C-in-C. Omar Pasha initially organized the successful defence of the Turkish fortresses along the Danube and later deployed some 30,000 of his men on the Crimean peninsula. These were mainly used in static defences, like the redoubts along the Causeway Heights which would figure so prominently in the Battle of Balaclava. Turks also defended Eupatoria, the town near the Calamita Bay landing beaches north of Sevastopol, and contributed to the defence of the Allied right flank in cooperation with the French Corps of Observation on the Sapoune Ridge. (David Paul)

▲Marshal St. Arnaud. The French Commander-in-Chief, who had made his reputation in suppressing colonial unrest in North Africa, proved an impatient colleague for Raglan. He impetuously sailed off before the main armada was ready to leave Bulgaria, then unexpectedly tried to postpone the landing until 1855, even though the whole Allied force was at sea en route for the Crimea. He contracted cholera shortly after the Battle of the Alma, took no positive part in the debate about whether or not to execute the 'flank march' and died soon after the Allies reached the Uplands south of Sevastopol. (David Paul)

That was all very well. Even if the ranks had not been ravaged by disease, there were two crucial obstacles facing the Allies: very little information was to hand about the size of the Russian forces in the Crimea (variously estimated at between 45,000 and 120,000). Second, no invasion plan existed. There was, too, always the need to act in consort with the French and Turks – never easy.

The first task was to agree a landing beach. On Raglan's behalf, Sir George Brown and the French General Canrobert examined the west coast of the Crimea, deciding on the mouth of the River Katcha, seven miles north of Sevastopol. So, once cholera had subsided in the fleets, the Allied armada was ordered to concentrate on Balchik Bay, south of Verna, during the first week of September. Its departure was not a model of organization. Impatiently, the French commander Marshal St. Arnaud set off in the sailing ship *Ville de Paris* two days before the main force, which eventually got under way on 7 September. Because both steam- and sail-powered ships were involved, with different speeds, the fleet was likely to straggle. Hence, a rendezvous was arranged off the mouth of the Danube before the final crossing of the Black Sea to the Crimea.

En route for the Danube, Raglan in the steamship *Caradoc* came up with St. Arnaud, who now favoured a landing on the east, not west, coast of the peninsula – and, quite astonishingly, in 1855 rather than in 1854. Resolved to be done with such nonsense, Raglan undertook a reconnaissance of his own. Instead of the Katcha, he chose Calamita Bay, eight miles south of the small port of Eupatoria (which on 13 September would be the first Allied conquest in the Crimea). This had a four-mile stretch of sand, shallow enough for artillery rafts to be towed ashore. An enemy frontal attack on the beach was prevented by two salt lakes, which also effectively narrowed the scope of any hostile action against the flanks. Naval gunfire could deal with low hills to the south and inland beyond the lakes.

Invasion of the Crimea

Thus, in Eupatoria Bay the Allied landings began shortly after dawn on 14 September – unopposed. Russian observers kept their distance; unknown to the Allies, their forces were massing in a strong position on the banks of the River Alma between them and their objective. The Russians would fight there on ground of their own choosing from prepared defences. They felt no need to interfere with the landings, therefore. At first, indeed, the landings did go smoothly. But before the 14th was out, rain and gales began to lash the exposed shore. Not for five days were the 20,000 troops and their equipment completely ashore. At length, on 19 September, before choking heat and dust silenced them, bands led the Allies south from the bridgehead. By mid-afternoon, many of those marching had collapsed from fatigue or illness and the Light Cavalry Brigade (the Heavy Brigade being still in Bulgaria) very nearly fell into an ambush beyond the tiny River Bulganek, where the Russian 17th Division lurked in dead ground.

Next day, however, the Allied troops, advancing with the French and Turks on the right near the sea, were forced into a major battle at the Alma, where the Russians had concentrated strong formations on hills astride the post road to Sevastopol. Attacking two redoubts across the river and up a steep slope on the enemy right, the British suffered heavy casualties. Eventually they carried the day, as further west French gunners turned the Russian left. By late afternoon the way to Sevastopol, the objective of the invasion, was open. But 362 British soldiers lay dead, while another 1,640 were wounded. For three days, the Allies were too exhausted to push on. By the time they did, the Russians had recovered their poise.

The naval port of Sevastopol was effectively divided in two by a large bay. Capture of the northern area itself, therefore, did not guarantee the fall of the dockyard facilities and the main town to the south. The Allies (who had not previously considered how they would actually *take* Sevastopol once they reached it) were faced with a serious dilemma: to attack the north, under the guns of the southern fortifications, anchored fleet and northern defences; or to march around Sevastopol to the uplands south of it. In other words, would it be better to outflank the city to the east and exert pressure directly on the dockyards to the south? This would eliminate the need to occupy the northern suburbs and afterwards cross the wide bay under fire. As the Allies had no boats with which to carry out such a perilous manoeuvre, it might well prove disastrous. So they decided to execute the so-called 'flank march' and attack from the south.

The Russians, meanwhile, had not been idle. Prince Menshikov, their commander-in-chief, decided to withdraw the fleet into harbour and sink blockships across the entrance. Naval guns and crews would be off-loaded to reinforce surrounding fortifications, which were rapidly and effectively being improved under the guidance of Colonel Todleben. Leaving some 16,000 militia, sailors and a few regular troops to guard Sevastopol, Menshikov then marched the bulk of his men eastwards beyond the River Tchernaya. There, he reasoned, they would pose an active menace to the exposed Allied flank, while being able at the same

The Landing and Advance to Sevastopol, 14-26 Sept 1854

time to receive reinforcements from across the Sea of Azov and via the Perekop peninsula in the north.

Quite ignorant of these movements, the Allies began their march around Sevastopol. On the way, they ran across the Russian rearguard leaving Sevastopol. Leading the advance, Raglan very nearly met the enemy quite ludicrously supported only by his ADCs. His cavalry escort had become temporarily lost. Fortunately unseen, the British commander-in-chief eased himself back to safety.

Next day, 26 September, the British came in sight of Balaclava. Little did they know that they would remain there for nearly two years and that it would give its name to a series of actions which would achieve lasting fame in the annals of British military history.

▶ Sevastopol from the sea. On the deck of the British warship stands an 87cwt pivot gun, capable of firing an 8in solid shot. Behind are the batteries of Sevastopol, ranged on both sides of the harbour entrance. (Sandhurst)

▲ *The River Bulganek. On the afternoon of 19 September 1854, the Light Brigade reached the Bulganek. About to attack Russian troops in front of it, the squadrons were recalled because of enemy infantry lying in wait for them in dead ground beyond the stream. The concealed Russians are in the background. (Sandhurst)*

◄ *Sevastopol. In the distance are the rolling hills beyond the River Tchernaya, which the Allies had to negotiate when marching round Sevastopol. The southern uplands, from which the Allies would mount their siege, are on the right. The formidable batteries are, from left to right: north of the harbour, North Fort, Telegraph Battery, Fort Constantine (114 guns); south of the harbour, Fort Nicholas (192 guns), Fort Alexander (64 guns) and Quarantine Battery (51 guns). (David Paul)*

◄North side of Sevastopol. On the far left, the Allied fleet is shown off the harbour entrance, across which the line of sunken ships appears. The rugged nature of the northern part of Sevastopol (whose batteries can be seen in the middle distance) illustrates how difficult it would have been for the Allies to cross the bay under fire from the south had they not elected to execute the 'flank march'. (Sandhurst)

◄Head of Sevastopol Harbour. On the high ground in the right foreground is an English mortar battery, overlooking the mouth of the River Tchernaya in the centre. A Russian battery across the bay is in the middle distance. To the left, on the dominating cliff stands the Inkerman West light. The Allies marched round the head of the harbour to the right of this scene during the 'flank march'. (Sandhurst)

◄Ruins of Inkerman. The ruins of Inkerman and the so-called City of Caverns east of the River Tchernaya, as it flowed into Sevastopol harbour. Once more the harsh nature of the terrain is clear. The Allies skirted this land to the east during the 'flank march'. (Sandhurst)

▶ *Kamiesch. When the British took Balaclava as their supply port, the French made use of Kamiesch on the southern side of Sevastopol Bay west of the Sevastopol harbour entrance nearer the Black Sea. The harbour of Kamiesch, as can be seen, was wider, and access to it by land and sea was much less tortuous than at Balaclava. (Sandhurst)*

▼ *Balaclava Harbour. A rather romantic portrayal of Balaclava harbour, looking from the gorge to Kadikoi out to sea, shortly after the British arrival. Neither the wharves, nor the harbour itself, are crowded as they would soon be. Note the variety of sailing and steam vessels already at anchor. (Sandhurst)*

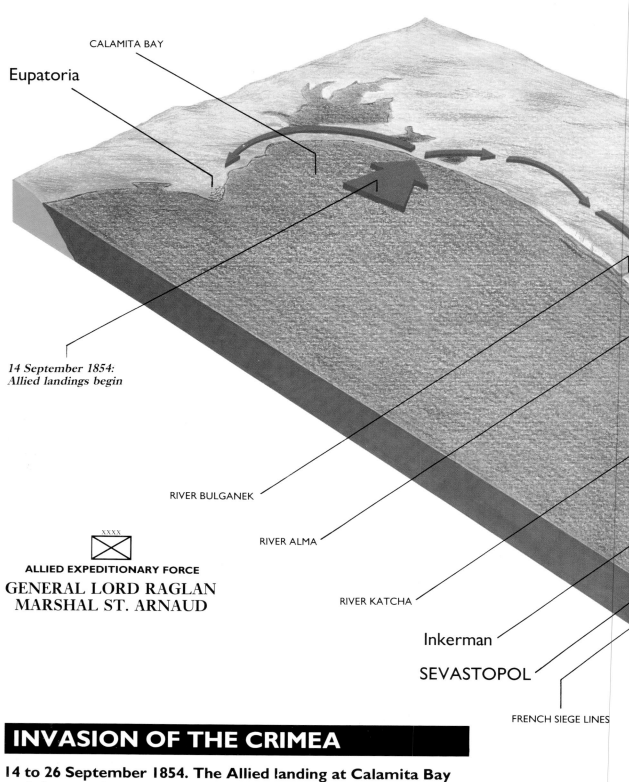

CALAMITA BAY

Eupatoria

14 September 1854:
Allied landings begin

XXXX

ALLIED EXPEDITIONARY FORCE
GENERAL LORD RAGLAN
MARSHAL ST. ARNAUD

RIVER BULGANEK

RIVER ALMA

RIVER KATCHA

Inkerman

SEVASTOPOL

FRENCH SIEGE LINES

INVASION OF THE CRIMEA

**14 to 26 September 1854. The Allied landing at Calamita Bay
and the march to Balaclava and Sevastopol.**

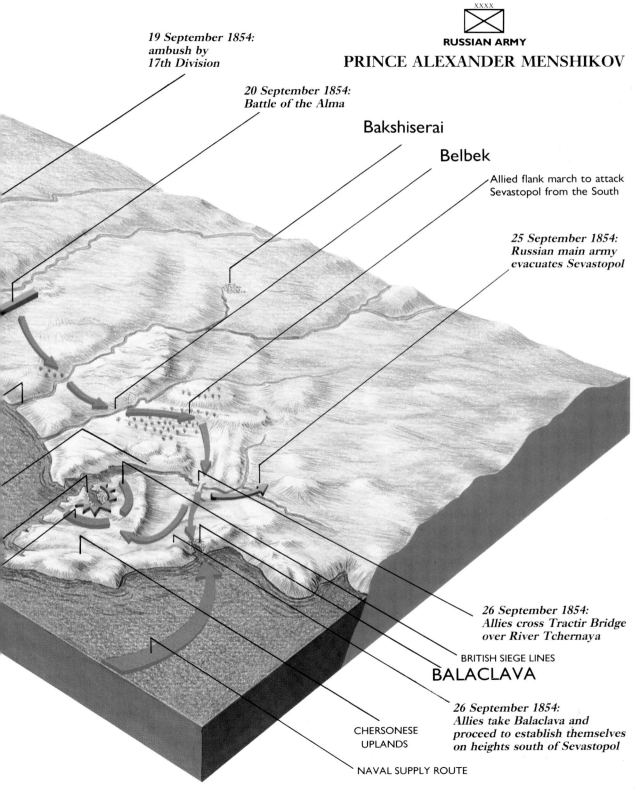

19 September 1854:
ambush by
17th Division

20 September 1854:
Battle of the Alma

XXXX

RUSSIAN ARMY

PRINCE ALEXANDER MENSHIKOV

Bakshiserai

Belbek

Allied flank march to attack
Sevastopol from the South

25 September 1854:
Russian main army
evacuates Sevastopol

26 September 1854:
Allies cross Tractir Bridge
over River Tchernaya

BRITISH SIEGE LINES

BALACLAVA

26 September 1854:
Allies take Balaclava and
proceed to establish themselves
on heights south of Sevastopol

CHERSONESE
UPLANDS

NAVAL SUPPLY ROUTE

PRELUDE TO BATTLE

Descending from hills east of Sevastopol, where it had bivouacked overnight, Lord Raglan's force crossed the Tchernaya by Tractir Bridge before advancing over the Fedioukine Hills and Causeway Heights on to the Plain of Balaclava – areas that would figure prominently in the battle a month later. Moving south of the small village of Kadikoi towards Balaclava, Raglan was fired on by a mortar from the old Genoese fort guarding the mouth of the harbour. Hastily taking cover, he ordered men of the Rifle Brigade to occupy heights east of Balaclava and capture the fort, but before they could do so, salvoes from the fleet, which had unnoticed arrived offshore, persuaded the fort's commander to surrender. He had, after all, preserved his military honour by offering token resistance.

So the British took possession of the tiny bay that would be their supply port for the duration of the Crimean War. Next day the French began to ascend the uplands south of Sevastopol, taking the ports of Kamisech and Kazatch west of the city. And, very shortly afterwards, the Allies settled down to besiege Sevastopol, the French on the left and the British on the right, with more French and Turkish troops guarding the right flank from the Sapoune Ridge 700 feet above the Plain of Balaclava.

Balaclava

The port of Balaclava was small and its approach from the sea difficult. Vessels having negotiated its narrow entrance must then manoeuvre sharply right and left to the wharves, which, although extended by engineers, remained woefully inadequate. The inner and outer harbours together stretched a mere 1,200 yards by 300 yards at the widest; and the entire complex resembled a thin 'J' with a small tail-like extension. To the west the

ground rose sharply: unloading there was out of the question. Only a maximum 600 yards of seafront on a narrow shelf to the east, therefore, could be used. A track then wound itself from the head of the bay through a steep gorge to Kadikoi, 754 feet above sea level, before turning due west along the South Valley to a 1:15 incline through the Col of Balaclava on to the Chersonese Uplands. In September, the going underfoot along this difficult track was firm. Nobody anticipated having to stay there for the winter, let alone two winters. The restricted size of Balaclava (into which countless British ships must crowd to unload and for shelter) and the tortuous path along which supplies of food and ammunition, equipment, horses and men must climb did not seem inadequate for a short campaign. Sevastopol would, surely, soon fall.

On a rocky prominence 469 feet above sea level, commanding the entrance to Balaclava harbour as it turned sharply right, was the fort that had briefly offered resistance on 26 September. East of Balaclava, and below the South Valley, were the low hills Raglan had ordered the Rifle Brigade to occupy preparatory to an assault on the castle. Rather optimistically, their peak was known locally as Mount Hiblak. They jutted 1½ miles

▶ *Top: Balaclava Harbour. This shows the port in 1855, once the wharves had been improved. Note the light railway running along the quay. This carried supplies up to the troops before Sevastopol, having been constructed by civilian contractors. (Sandhurst)*

Below: A closer look at the crowded harbour and inadequate wharves. Despite the pressure on berths, Lord Cardigan was given permission to keep his yacht in Balaclava harbour. He was in the habit of sleeping there to avoid the discomforts of the camp. He did so during the night of 24/25 October and was not therefore with the Light Brigade at the beginning of the Battle of Balaclava. (Selby)

◀ Officer, 42nd Highlanders, a regiment in the Highland Brigade of the British First Infantry Division which descended to the North Valley from the Sapoune Ridge via the Woronzov Road. The 42nd and 79th Regiments remained on the Plain under Sir Colin Campbell's command to reinforce the defences of Balaclava after the battle.

▶ Sergeant, 2nd (Royal North British) Dragoons – The Scots Greys. This regiment's two squadrons under Lieutenant-Colonel Henry Griffith charged the centre of the main body of Russian cavalry in the Heavy Brigade's attack on General Ryzhov's force as it advanced over the Causeway Heights towards Kadikoi.

▲ Corporal, 93rd Highlanders. This regiment under Sir Colin Campbell occupied the rise north of Kadikoi from which the initial Russian cavalry attack by four squadrons was repulsed in the action of 'The Thin Red Line'.

▶A closer view of the defences of Sevastopol, seen from the centre of the Allied line. The puffs of smoke to left and right in the middle distance show respectively French and British batteries in action. The large building in the centre of the picture is Fort Constantine on the northern side of the harbour entrance. The British fleet is off shore. Wagons wending their way up the rough track in the foreground illustrate the crude supply line operating in the autumn of 1854. Note, too, the pack mule. (Sandhurst)

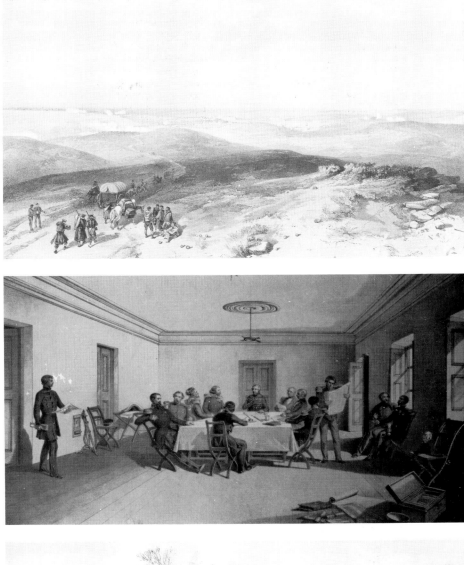

▶Lord Raglan's Headquarters. Lord Raglan established his headquarters in a farm, which had extensive outbuildings, on the Chersonese Uplands close to the Col of Balaclava. Situated behind the British divisional camps, the headquarters lay just over 4 miles from Balaclava. In this scene, Raglan at the head of the table is engaged in what the artist calls 'A Council of War'. (Sandhurst)

▶An external view of Lord Raglan's headquarters on the Chersonese Uplands. The artist intends to portray the constant comings and goings associated with an Allied HQ engaged in conducting operations in a theatre of war. (Sandhurst)

▲Lord Raglan's headquarters complex is in the centre of this scene, the large white building being Raglan's own quarters. Smoke in the distance represents French batteries firing on the left, British in the centre. Beyond Sevastopol is the British fleet offshore. In the foreground stands Captain Brandling's troop of horse artillery. Other British divisional camps are depicted in the right background. Just beyond Brandling's troop is the Heavy Brigade camp, whence Scarlett was to move after the Battle of Balaclava. (Sandhurst)

▼This is the view of Sevastopol from the extreme right of the British trenches. Note the size of the port, which was not so evident from a central position on the Uplands. Naval vessels in the harbour were used to enhance the fire of the static defences. (Sandhurst)

north-east to another gorge, which separated them from more heights surrounding the village of Kamara. Beyond them, some three miles further east, lay the Baidar Valley where part of the Russian force involved in the Battle of Balaclava would form up.

Parallel to the sea, immediately north of Kadikoi, which lay 1¾ miles above the head of Balaclava harbour, and at right-angles to it stood South Valley, almost four miles from west to east and just short of a mile north-south. In turn, it was bordered to the north by the Causeway Heights (approximately 300 feet high) along which ran for part of its length the metalled Woronzov Road. Halfway along, this road dipped to the floor of the adjacent North Valley before climbing again up the escarpment of the Sapoune Ridge on its way to Sevastopol. The North Valley (running from the

▲ His Highness Prince Alexander S. Menshikov. General-Adjutant and Admiral, Commander-in-Chief of Russian forces in the Crimea, Menshikov assured the Tsar that he could hold the line of the River Alma for at least three weeks to enable strengthening of the defences of Sevastopol. He therefore had to conceal the real nature of the reverse from Nicholas I. The Tsar, anxious for evidence of victory, pressed Menshikov, against his better judgement, to launch the attack on 25 October. The plan that Menshikov devised was too complicated and, when it failed, again the Commander-in-Chief effectively misled the Tsar in his post-operational dispatch. Eventually, when no clear success had been offered to him, the Tsar dismissed Menshikov in February 1855. (Warner)

▲Colonel E. I. Todleben. Commander of the engineers in Sevastopol, he was chiefly responsible for strengthening the southern defences once it became clear that the Allies intended to attack the naval port from that direction. Sir George Cathcart reputedly dismissed the defences as little more than 'a low park wall', when he arrived on the Chersonese Uplands. Even if this were an exaggeration, there were very few redoubts then in a good state of repair. Todleben laboured quickly and successfully to produce defences that would defy the combined Allied might for almost exactly a year. Then the Russians would voluntarily retire across Sevastopol Bay to the northern suburbs. (Selby)

Sapoune Ridge to another group of hills abutting the River Tchernaya) stretched three miles west-east and 1½ miles north-south, being bounded on the north by a collection of low rises collectively called the Fedioukine Hills.

In the area of Chorgun, north-eastwards across the Tchernaya and due east beyond Kamara, was the Russian field army, which had marched out of Sevastopol. If the flanks of the entrenched Allied troops on the Chersonese Uplands south of Sevastopol needed to be covered by additional French and Turkish troops, so did Balaclava require special protection. Without succour by this route, the British effort must wither, the Allied siege of Sevastopol fail. Yet, in reality, because of sickness and the overriding priority of the siege operations, there were relatively few men available to guard Balaclava against possible Russian attack from three directions. Like the Allies, the enemy might cross the Tchernaya (which ran north-west into Sevastopol Bay about five miles east of Balaclava) over the Tractir Bridge, advancing southwards across the Fedioukine Hills and into the North Valley. They might however, use either or both of two fords lower down the Tchernaya, pass under the nearby aqueduct and gain direct entry to the eastern end of North Valley. From there they could sweep over the Causeway Heights before reinforcements could descend from the Sapoune Ridge. Third,

▲ The Redan. This contemporary print shows what one of Todleben's major defence works (the Redan) looked like from an advanced British parallel. Twice during 1855 the British would be bloodily repulsed from it. (David Paul)

though perhaps less likely, owing to the rugged nature of the ground, the enemy might strike in force west from Kamara. The second of these options posed the most acute danger. An advance over Tractir Bridge would be detected early enough to permit troops to use the Col and Woronzov Road descents from the Uplands swiftly enough to block their path. But the more northerly of the fords at the end of the North Valley carried the road (little more than a track) from Balaclava to Bakshi Serai in the interior. The southern one, although wider and with a steeper approach, led virtually straight on to the Causeway Heights and the Woronzov Road, which topped it.

Allied Defences

The potential of an enemy advance into the North Valley was quickly recognized, and six redoubts were built along the crest of the Causeway Heights. The redoubts were simply numbered 1 to 6 from east to west. Five were spread over two miles (and thus roughly 500 yards apart, although No. 4 lay 800 yards from No. 3) at right-angles to Balaclava harbour. The sixth lay on a detached

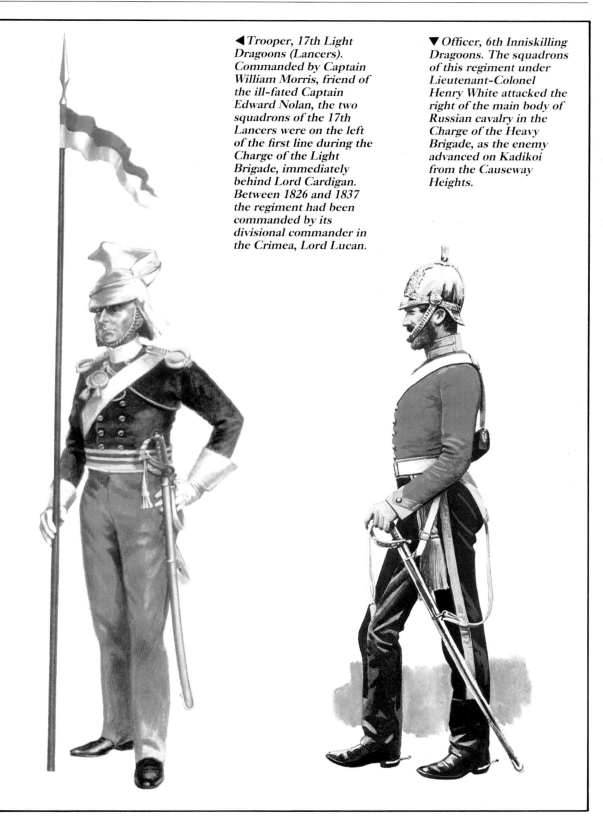

◄Trooper, 17th Light Dragoons (Lancers). Commanded by Captain William Morris, friend of the ill-fated Captain Edward Nolan, the two squadrons of the 17th Lancers were on the left of the first line during the Charge of the Light Brigade, immediately behind Lord Cardigan. Between 1826 and 1837 the regiment had been commanded by its divisional commander in the Crimea, Lord Lucan.

▼Officer, 6th Inniskilling Dragoons. The squadrons of this regiment under Lieutenant-Colonel Henry White attacked the right of the main body of Russian cavalry in the Charge of the Heavy Brigade, as the enemy advanced on Kadikoi from the Causeway Heights.

◀Diamond Battery. Captioned 'A Quiet Day', this shows the 'Diamond' battery, whose Lancaster 68-pounder gun's crew were from HMS Diamond. Captain Peel stands in the centre; Commander Burnet is beside him with the telescope. 12-pounder guns from HMS Diamond were used in the redoubts along the Causeway Heights. (Sandhurst)

◀Batteries in Action. In contrast to the 'quiet day' depicted in the 'Diamond' Battery, this shows 'a hot day'. On the extreme left, the Woronzov Road (which went across the Causeway Heights and figured prominently in the Battle of Balaclava) runs to the head of Dockyard Creek in Sevastopol. The line running across the centre is the Second Parallel, and on the far

right lies the troublesome Malakov defence-work. When this fell in September 1855, Sevastopol south of the Bay was compromised; and the Russians withdrew to the north of the Bay. (Sandhurst)

▶ A quiet night in the batteries; but note the obvious cold. The look-outs are muffled, gunners keep warm round a fire and in the background other figures are huddled in shelter. (Sandhurst)

▼No need to huddle together for warmth during this night. Clearly this is warm work. Note the ammunition party arriving on the right and the different stages of firing shown on the three guns. (Sandhurst)

▲Russian Defences. The trenches are those of the British right attack on the Uplands before Sevastopol. This scene also shows three of Todleben's defence-works, which caused the Allies infinite trouble and many casualties. In the centre, with the flag, is the Redan: on the hill to its right lies the Malakov and, on the extreme right, the flat work with no flag is the Mamelon. The British trenches, supplied from Balaclava, are about seven miles from the port. (Sandhurst)

▼Forward Defences. This shows British guns opposite the Mamelon defence-work (in the centre background). The nearer of the two mortars is a 10-inch weapon, the further a 13-inch. On the extreme right is the Lancaster battery. All the ammunition and stores, shown here, would have been brought up from Balaclava. (Sandhurst)

▼Left to right: Officer, Guardsman, Drummer and Colour Sergeant, The Grenadier Guards. The 3rd Battalion, Grenadier Guards, formed part of the Guards Brigade of Lieutenant-General HRH The Duke of Cambridge's First Division, which arrived on the Plain of Balaclava from the Sapoune Ridge after the Charge of the Light Brigade had ended.

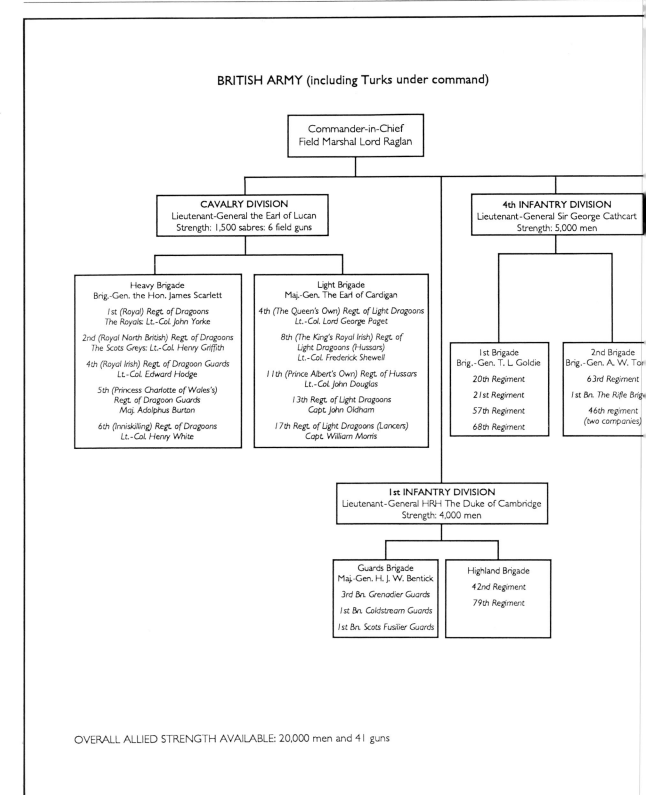

BRITISH ARMY (including Turks under command)

Commander-in-Chief
Field Marshal Lord Raglan

CAVALRY DIVISION
Lieutenant-General the Earl of Lucan
Strength: 1,500 sabres: 6 field guns

4th INFANTRY DIVISION
Lieutenant-General Sir George Cathcart
Strength: 5,000 men

Heavy Brigade
Brig.-Gen. the Hon. James Scarlett

*1st (Royal) Regt. of Dragoons
The Royals: Lt.-Col. John Yorke*

*2nd (Royal North British) Regt. of Dragoons
The Scots Greys: Lt.-Col. Henry Griffith*

*4th (Royal Irish) Regt. of Dragoon Guards
Lt.-Col. Edward Hodge*

*5th (Princess Charlotte of Wales's)
Regt. of Dragoon Guards
Maj. Adolphus Burton*

*6th (Inniskilling) Regt. of Dragoons
Lt.-Col. Henry White*

Light Brigade
Maj.-Gen. The Earl of Cardigan

*4th (The Queen's Own) Regt. of Light Dragoons
Lt.-Col. Lord George Paget*

*8th (The King's Royal Irish) Regt. of
Light Dragoons (Hussars)
Lt.-Col. Frederick Shewell*

*11th (Prince Albert's Own) Regt. of Hussars
Lt.-Col. John Douglas*

*13th Regt. of Light Dragoons
Capt. John Oldham*

*17th Regt. of Light Dragoons (Lancers)
Capt. William Morris*

1st Brigade
Brig.-Gen. T. L. Goldie

20th Regiment

21st Regiment

57th Regiment

68th Regiment

2nd Brigade
Brig.-Gen. A. W. Tor

63rd Regiment

1st Bn. The Rifle Brig

*46th regiment
(two companies)*

1st INFANTRY DIVISION
Lieutenant-General HRH The Duke of Cambridge
Strength: 4,000 men

Guards Brigade
Maj.-Gen. H. J. W. Bentick

3rd Bn. Grenadier Guards

1st Bn. Coldstream Guards

1st Bn. Scots Fusilier Guards

Highland Brigade

42nd Regiment

79th Regiment

OVERALL ALLIED STRENGTH AVAILABLE: 20,000 men and 41 guns

ALLIED ORDER OF BATTLE

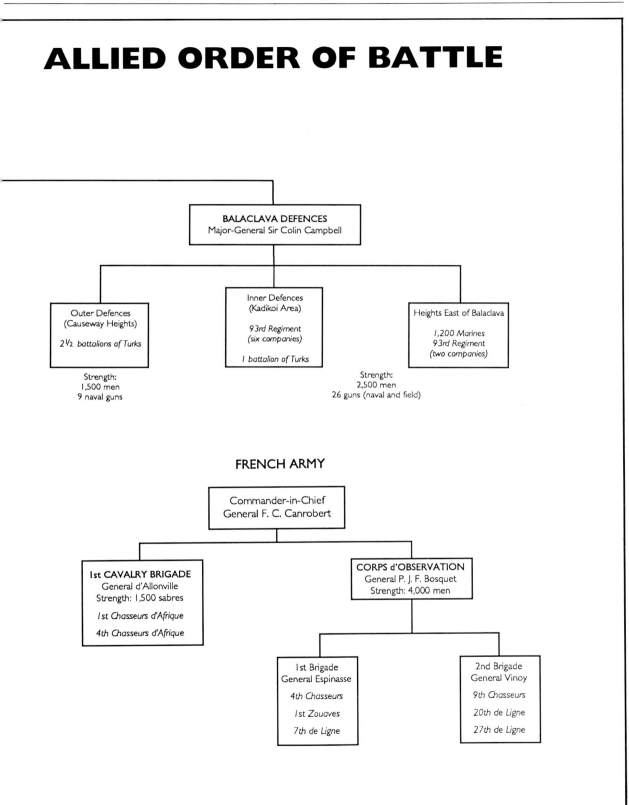

BALACLAVA DEFENCES
Major-General Sir Colin Campbell

Outer Defences
(Causeway Heights)

2½ battalions of Turks

Strength:
1,500 men
9 naval guns

Inner Defences
(Kadikoi Area)

93rd Regiment
(six companies)

1 battalion of Turks

Heights East of Balaclava

1,200 Marines
93rd Regiment
(two companies)

Strength:
2,500 men
26 guns (naval and field)

FRENCH ARMY

Commander-in-Chief
General F. C. Canrobert

1st CAVALRY BRIGADE
General d'Allonville
Strength: 1,500 sabres

1st Chasseurs d'Afrique

4th Chasseurs d'Afrique

CORPS d'OBSERVATION
General P. J. F. Bosquet
Strength: 4,000 men

1st Brigade
General Espinasse

4th Chasseurs

1st Zouaves

7th de Ligne

2nd Brigade
General Vinoy

9th Chasseurs

20th de Ligne

27th de Ligne

rise, 500 feet above sea level and known as Canrobert's Hill, almost 1,000 yards south-east of the easternmost redoubt along the Causeway Heights and 200 feet above it. No. 1 (on Canrobert's Hill) in theory covered any outflanking movement around the Causeway Heights to the east, and its garrison could also observe movement in the area of Kamara, 2,000 yards south-east.

Owing to the urgency of the situation, with the Russians likely to attack before the siege was fully under way, these redoubts were constructed quickly by Turks under British direction – No. 2 was reputedly raised in a single day. None were formidable defence-works. Only four of them were armed with 12-pounder naval guns, three of which were placed in No. 1, and two each in the next

Russian infantry private.

Hussar, Ingermanland Regiment.

▶ *Fourth Division Camp. Although on the Chersonese Uplands, from which Sir George Cathcart marched the division down to the Plain of Balaclava on 25 October 1854, this portrayal of the 4th Division's camp is clearly at a later date. Huts were not brought up until 1855. By then, Cathcart was dead – killed at the Battle of Inkerman on 5 November 1854. (Sandhurst)*

▶ *The crucial Tractir Bridge at a later stage of the campaign. It provided the best passage of the River Tchernaya. Over it the Allies passed on their way to Balaclava and many of the troops destined to take part in the Battle of Balaclava on 25 October 1854 crossed it in the darkness of that pre-dawn. (Mollo)*

▶*Kadikoi. A later scene, but showing the general area of Kadikoi village, looking south from the direction of the knoll on which 'The Thin Red Line' fought. The gorge to Balaclava is in the background. The passage of supplies along the rough track (note how deep the wheels of the wagon have sunk) towards the Col of Balaclava shows how vital this route was for British troops on the Chersonese Uplands. (Selby)*

three redoubts. Nos. 5 and 6 would be unfinished and therefore unmanned on 25 October. No. 1 had a battalion (roughly 600) of Turks in or around it, Nos. 2–4 a half-battalion. A British artillery NCO was in charge of each of the four redoubts. These fortifications, with their 1,500 men and nine 12-pounder guns, comprised the outer defences of Balaclava.

Just north of Kadikoi, covering access to the

▲ *General Pierre François Joseph Bosquet. A French divisional commander during the Battle of the Alma, Bosquet managed to turn the left of the enemy position close to the Black Sea, as the British attacked the main Russian force further inland on the road to Sevastopol. During the Battle of Balaclava, he was commander of the French 'Corps of Observation' guarding the Allied right flank on the Sapoune Ridge. Part of*

his force was sent down to the Plain by Canrobert. Watching the Charge of the Light Brigade from the Uplands, he made the famous remark: 'C'est magnifique, mais ce n'est pas la guerre.' (David Paul)

head of the gorge that led directly to wharves of Balaclava, the 93rd (Sutherland) Highlanders less two of its companies in Balaclava and another two stationed on the heights east of the port, but plus a battalion of Turks, were deployed on a prominent knoll. Nearby was Captain Barker's six-gun battery of field artillery. On the Mount Hiblak heights (later renamed Marine Heights), immediately to the east and north-east of Balaclava, and ready to counter an advance from Kamara, were 1,200 marines and the two detached companies of the 93rd. The inner defences at Kadikoi and on Mount Hiblak ran in a semicircle three miles long. In all, manned either by Royal Artillery or Marine Artillery personnel, they included 26 guns. Both inner and outer defences were under Sir Colin Campbell, who had led the Highland Brigade at the Alma and had considerable active service experience in India.

The bulk of General Bosquet's French 'Corps of Observation' was situated on the Sapoune Ridge above the Plain of Balaclava. The five British infantry divisions were beyond Bosquet on the Uplands. In Balaclava harbour lay a frigate, and up to 100 soldiers were on detached duty in the small port.

As an added mobile defence, the British Cavalry Division under Lord Lucan was encamped below No. 6 redoubt at the western end of the South Valley, 1½ miles north-west of Kadikoi. Both of its brigades (totalling some 1,500 men) were present, together with Captain Maude's supporting troop of horse artillery. The cavalry were not under Campbell, which made sense: Campbell's only responsibility was to defend Balaclava, while the cavalry must be free to act independently, if required.

Campbell was not unhappy about these arrangements. Five days before they were put to the test, although slightly apprehensive about a night attack on the redoubts, he reported to Raglan: 'I fancy we are now very strong as well as secure.' However, none of the redoubts would be able to withstand a determined assault without rapid reinforcement, which could only come from the cavalry under its independent commander. Troops on the Uplands before Sevastopol could not reach the Plain in time to prevent disaster.

RUSSIAN ORDER OF BATTLE

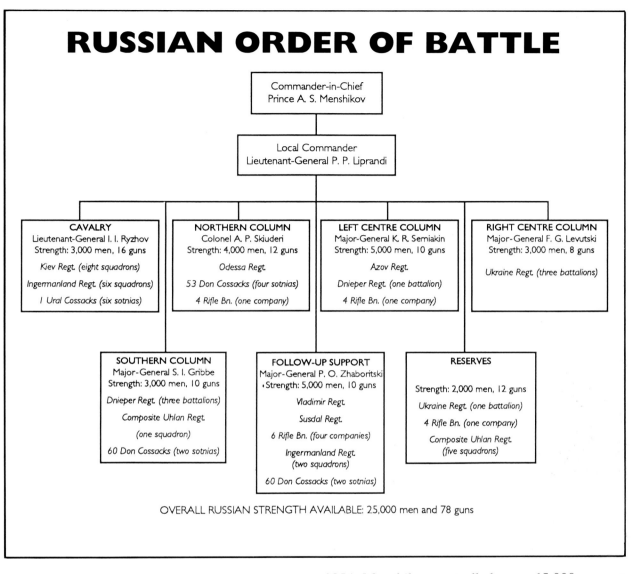

Commander-in-Chief
Prince A. S. Menshikov

Local Commander
Lieutenant-General P. P. Liprandi

CAVALRY
Lieutenant-General I. I. Ryzhov
Strength: 3,000 men, 16 guns

Kiev Regt. (eight squadrons)

Ingermanland Regt. (six squadrons)

I Ural Cossacks (six sotnias)

NORTHERN COLUMN
Colonel A. P. Skiuderi
Strength: 4,000 men, 12 guns

Odessa Regt.

53 Don Cossacks (four sotnias)

4 Rifle Bn. (one company)

LEFT CENTRE COLUMN
Major-General K. R. Semiakin
Strength: 5,000 men, 10 guns

Azov Regt.

Dnieper Regt. (one battalion)

4 Rifle Bn. (one company)

RIGHT CENTRE COLUMN
Major-General F. G. Levutski
Strength: 3,000 men, 8 guns

Ukraine Regt. (three battalions)

SOUTHERN COLUMN
Major-General S. I. Gribbe
Strength: 3,000 men, 10 guns

Dnieper Regt. (three battalions)

Composite Uhlan Regt.
(one squadron)

60 Don Cossacks (two sotnias)

FOLLOW-UP SUPPORT
Major-General P. O. Zhaboritski
Strength: 5,000 men, 10 guns

Vladimir Regt.

Susdal Regt.

6 Rifle Bn. (four companies)

Ingermanland Regt.
(two squadrons)

60 Don Cossacks (two sotnias)

RESERVES

Strength: 2,000 men, 12 guns

Ukraine Regt. (one battalion)

4 Rifle Bn. (one company)

Composite Uhlan Regt.
(five squadrons)

OVERALL RUSSIAN STRENGTH AVAILABLE: 25,000 men and 78 guns

Russian Menace

Across the Tchernaya, Prince Menshikov commanded a formidable array of troops, which had recently been reinforced by four regiments of Lieutenant-General P. P. Liprandi's 12th Infantry Division from Bessarabia. One other infantry regiment, a detached rifle battalion, seven further infantry battalions and five artillery batteries had also arrived early in October. The cavalry, under Lieutenant-General I. I. Ryzhov, had been similarly increased to two hussar, two lancer and two Cossack regiments, with the horse artillery also brought under his command. In all, on 24 October 1854, Menshikov controlled some 65,000 men, at a time when the Allies had scarcely more and were in the throes of trying to press the siege to a swift conclusion. The bulk of these forces were grouped around Chorgun: some 25 infantry battalions, 34 cavalry squadrons and 78 guns (20,000 infantry, 3,400 cavalry and 2,300 gunners). Including the British cavalry division, marines, Turks and Highlanders, the defenders of Balaclava totalled no more than 4,500 men; and they were also to guard the open flank between the supply port and the Baidar Valley by means of pickets and patrols.

Menshikov soon realized that his enemy's weakness on the flank was not Balaclava itself –

with defended heights guarding its eastern approaches and immediate access only through the narrow gorge south of Kadikoi – but the outer defences of the Causeway Heights and, further south, the village of Kadikoi. By capturing these, the Russians would cut the British lines of communication. Kadikoi was the key: with its loss to the Allies Balaclava would become effectively worthless. Russian reconnaissance patrols from the Baidar Valley on 18 and 19 October confirmed Menshikov's belief that the British outer defences

▶ *Barabanshchik of a Russian Infantry Regiment in summer parade dress, similar to that worn by Russian troops in the Crimea.*

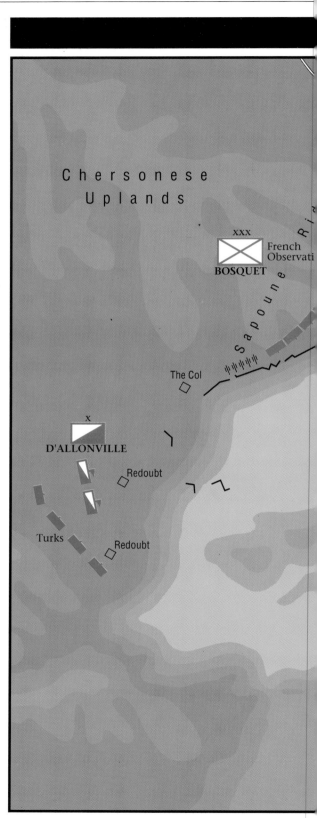

Defence of Balaclava and the Russian Plan

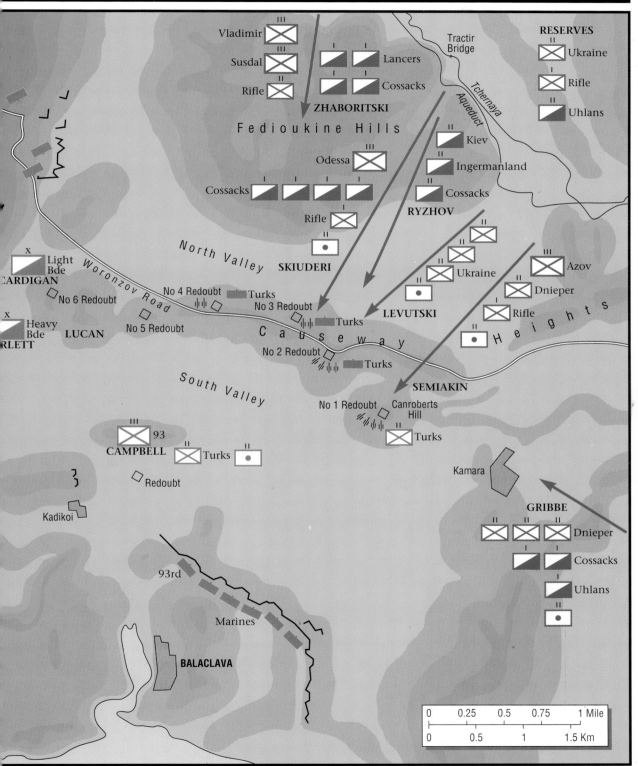

RESERVES

Vladimir

Susdal

Rifle

Lancers

Cossacks

ZHABORITSKI

F e d i o u k i n e   H i l l s

Ukraine

Rifle

Uhlans

Kiev

Ingermanland

Cossacks

RYZHOV

Odessa

Cossacks

Rifle

SKIUDERI

N o r t h   V a l l e y

Tractir
Bridge

Tchernaya

Aqueduct

Ukraine

Azov

Dnieper

Rifle

LEVUTSKI

H e i g h t s

x
Light
Bde
CARDIGAN

No 6 Redoubt

W o r o n z o v   R o a d

No 4 Redoubt

No 5 Redoubt

Turks

No 3 Redoubt

Turks

C a u s e w a y

No 2 Redoubt

Turks

SEMIAKIN

x
Heavy
Bde
RLETT

LUCAN

S o u t h   V a l l e y

No 1 Redoubt

Canroberts
Hill

Turks

93

CAMPBELL

Turks

Redoubt

Kadikoi

Kamara

GRIBBE

Dnieper

Cossacks

Uhlans

93rd

Marines

BALACLAVA

| 0 | 0.25 | 0.5 | 0.75 | 1 Mile |
| 0 | 0.5 | 1 | 1.5 Km | |

43

were weak. Against them, therefore, he planned a three-pronged attack, which he entrusted to Liprandi.

On the Russian left (the southern prong), Major-General S. I. Gribbe was to advance westwards with three battalions of the Dnieper infantry regiment, part of a Composite Uhlan (Lancer) Regiment (formed from reserves originally intended to boost other light cavalry units), some Cossacks and artillery support. The infantry would take the village of Kamara (2½ miles due east of Kadikoi) and the surrounding high ground, while the cavalry overran a monastery further south in which British pickets were posted. Direct pressure could then be applied to No. 1 redoubt.

In the centre, Major-General K. R. Semiakin would cross the Tchernaya from Chorgun a mile further north towards Kadikoi. This force would consist of two columns: Semiakin himself would lead that on the left with the Azov Regiment and one battalion of the Dnieper plus artillery support; Major-General F. G. Levutski would meanwhile take charge of the right column of the Ukraine Regiment and eight guns. These troops would cross the Tchernaya east of North Valley and converge on redoubts Nos. 1 and 2.

The northern prong (Russian right), commanded by Colonel A. P. Skiuderi and comprising the Odessa Regiment, 53rd Don Cossack Regiment with artillery support, would drive British

▲ Lieutenant-General P. P. Liprandi. Commander of the Russian 12th Infantry Division, Liprandi coordinated the three-pronged attack across the Tchernaya on 25 October 1854. He was responsible for the execution, not formulation, of the operational plan. Moreover, it was no fault of his that the Russian cavalry acted so indecisively during the Battle of Balaclava. He did capture the outer defences of Balaclava, inflict a clear defeat on the Light Brigade – if loss of horses and men be the criterion for success – and register territorial gain. His post-operational dispatch (further enhanced by Menshikov) was optimistic. But he could, on the whole, be satisfied with the day's achievements. Liprandi was to command a corps later in the campaign. (Selby)

▲ Major-General K. R. Semiakin. A brigade commander in the Russian 12th Infantry Division, Semiakin led the central force of the three-pronged attack during the Battle of Balaclava. With a combined force of nine infantry battalions, with artillery support, he and Major-General Levutski crossed the Tchernaya from Chorgun towards Nos. 1 and 2 redoubts on the Causeway Heights. Semiakin stormed Canrobert's Hill with the five battalions under his direct command and was therefore largely responsible for carrying the outer line of Balaclava's defences. Promoted after the British had been repulsed from The Redan in June 1855, Semiakin commanded Russian forces in the old town of Sevastopol during the Allies' final attack in September. (Selby)

pickets from Tractir Bridge and advance on No. 3 redoubt. In its wake Ryzhov was to advance with fourteen squadrons of hussars, a Ural Cossack regiment and two artillery batteries – in fact, the main body of cavalry. Once the redoubts had been taken Ryzhov would attack British positions around Kadikoi. Initially, however, he would concentrate at the eastern end of North Valley to await further orders. Behind Ryzhov, one battalion of the Ukraine Regiment, a company of riflemen and one field battery were left to guard the crucial Tractir Bridge. No other reserves were readily available.

To protect the right flank of the entire attack from interference by troops on the Sapoune Ridge,

Major-General O. P. Zhaboritski was to march a combined infantry, cavalry and artillery force of some 5,000 men from beyond the Tchernaya to occupy the Fedioukine Hills.

All these troops began to move forward as darkness fell. Liprandi watched while the northern prong crossed Tractir Bridge, then rode south to the eastern end of the North Valley and on to the Baidar Valley to encourage the other forces.

Late on the evening of 24 October a spy brought details of Liprandi's plans to the Turkish commander, Rustem Pasha: 25,000 men would attack next morning. After carefully examining the evidence, Lord Lucan and Sir Colin Campbell decided that the information was genuine. They

▲ *Major-General F. G. Levutski. A brigade commander of the Russian 12th Infantry Division, Levutski led four infantry battalions and a field battery of eight guns as part of the central force in the attack across the Tchernaya towards Kadikoi on 25 October. Under Major-General Semiakin's control, and in cooperation with him, he attacked the Causeway Heights and deployed his men in possession of the* Woronzov Road, which ran along the Heights, once Turkish garrisons in the redoubts had fled. His guns were among those to fire with such effect on the Light Brigade in its advance down the North Valley. (Selby)

▲ *Colonel Prince A. V. Obolenski. Commander of the Don Cossack field battery, whose eight guns were drawn up across the eastern end of the North Valley, Obolenski was talking to the cavalry commander, Lieutenant-General I. I. Ryzhov just after 11am on 25 October when his gunners spotted the approach of the Light Brigade. Before it was overrun, his battery caused considerable damage in the British* ranks. Not all of the gunners fled, and strenuous efforts were made to save the guns. They were not taken by the British, and therefore Obolenski could claim credit for a relatively successful action. (Selby) alerted Lord Raglan at his headquarters in a letter carried by one of Lucan's ADCs (his son, Lord Bingham). Unfortunately, a similar report had arrived a few days earlier, and on 21 October 1,000 men of the British 4th Division had been marched down to the Plain as the Cavalry Division turned out during a bitterly cold night in which one officer had died of exposure. It was all in vain: nothing hostile happened. This time, during the night of 24/25 October, Raglan took no such action. Apparently, on receiving the Turkish spy's report shortly before midnight, he suspected more false information. 'Very well', he murmured.

At dawn on 25 October all would be far from well. The opening shots in the Battle of Balaclava were about to be fired.

Junior officer, French Chasseurs d'Afrique.

Turkish officer.

PHASE I
FALL OF THE REDOUBTS

At 5am, an hour before dawn on 25 October, the British Cavalry Division was already standing to its horses. The camps of the two brigades lay close together in the South Valley below No. 6 redoubt, the Heavy Brigade slightly nearer the Causeway Heights and north-east of the Light Brigade.

Leaving the squadrons thus prepared, Lord Lucan with his staff and Lord George Paget from the Light Brigade cantered across the South Valley towards the Kamara Heights where a cavalry picket had been posted. As the sky lightened in the east, a staff officer pointed out two flags, one above the other, flying over No. 1 redoubt on Canrobert's Hill – the signal for 'enemy advancing'. Almost simultaneously, as the flags became clearer a gun boomed from the redoubt. That settled any lingering doubt. The fortification was under attack. Lucan's ADCs spurred back to divisional headquarters as Paget returned to the Light Brigade, of which he was in command until Lord Cardigan came up after spending the night aboard his yacht in Balaclava harbour.

Joined by Sir Colin Campbell, Lucan remained in the eastern part of South Valley, and both officers started to assess the situation. Deciding that this was no nuisance pinprick raid, Lucan sent Captain Charteris to warn Lord Raglan on the Chersonese Uplands. Campbell returned to his troops near Kadikoi, and Lucan rode westwards once more. Putting the Light Brigade in reserve, Lucan led the Heavy Brigade back east. With no intention of engaging the enemy infantry, he flamboyantly manoeuvred the brigade, hoping to dissuade the Russians from further advance, while Captain Maude took his six field guns on to the Causeway Heights to the right of No. 3 redoubt. Unfortunately, the enemy was neither impressed nor deterred.

At almost precisely the same moment that the British cavalry stood to their horses, the Russian advance began. Gribbe led the three Dnieper battalions, lancers, Cossacks, six light field pieces and four heavier cannon out of the Baidar Valley towards Kamara, as planned. An hour later, having taken the pickets by surprise, they were in possession of Kamara and, more critically, the high ground around it which overlooked the South Valley. In the centre, with four battalions of the Azov Regiment, the fourth battalion of the Dnieper Regiment, a rifle company and the same artillery strength as Gribbe, Semiakin gained the slopes north and north-east of No. 1 redoubt unopposed. On his right, Levutski's three Ukraine battalions moved on No. 2 redoubt as his cannon opened fire on Nos. 2 and 3 redoubts. Having crossed the Tractir Bridge, leading the northern prong of the attack, Skiuderi aimed for No. 3 redoubt with the four Odessa battalions, three Cossack squadrons and a field battery. Thus far Menshikov could be well satisfied with progress. They were all on schedule.

When Levutski began to bombard Nos. 2 and 3 redoubts at 6am, Gribbe ranged his ten guns along the edge of the Kamara Heights on No. 1. Further north, Semiakin's ten also joined in. Under cover of this barrage the 600 Turks, in their low breastwork with its salient jutting to the north-east, saw eight infantry battalions converging on them from the north and east. The defenders had not helped their cause by failing to clear bushes and scrub around the redoubt, which gave valuable cover to the preceding skirmishers. As the infantry of Gribbe and Semiakin advanced, they were fired upon (apart from optimistic small arms shots at extreme range) by just eleven Allied guns: five in Nos. 1 and 2 redoubts and Maude's field battery. Soon, however, Maude's battery was withdrawn. The commander himself was 'horribly wounded', in the words of one eyewitness, as a shell shattered the innards of his horse. His gunners were also running short of ammunition – in their haste to get into action, they had failed to bring with them full limber support. Learning that there were only sufficient shells left for one gun, Lucan ordered the battery out of the line.

The position of No. 1 redoubt was now perilous. Unable to compete with the enemy shell-fire, the Turks withdrew to the relatively un-scathed western end of their fortification to await the inevitable infantry assault. It was not long coming. Deploying his riflemen in advance and under cover of his artillery, Semiakin personally directed the storming of Canrobert's Hill. First he sent in three battalions of the Azov Regiment in two lines 100 yards apart, followed by a third line comprising the remaining Azov battalion and one from the Dnieper Regiment 150 yards further back. After advancing steadily uphill under desul-tory fire, 100 yards from the summit they charged the defence-work. Meeting little resistance, the battalions dashed through the shallow ditch and over the low parapet. There the remnants of the Turkish garrison were overwhelmed. Reports of scant resistance and 'not much determination' inside the redoubt suggest that many of the 170 killed there may have, in biblical terms, simply been put to the sword. Before escaping, the British NCO in command of the redoubt managed to spike the three guns so that they could not be turned and used by the Russians against the Allies. Nevertheless, at 7.30am the Azov flag was run up. The first of the outer fortifications of Balaclava had fallen.

Only Maude's field battery had come to the aid of the Turks, and that to little real effect. Neither infantry nor cavalry had made a serious move to help. Faced with the advance of Levutski and Skiuderi's eight battalions with artillery and cavalry support, the garrisons of the other three defended redoubts (Nos. 2, 3 and 4) voted with their feet – they fled, as one observer put it 'with their quilts and the rest of their simple camp treasures . . . Coming west with these burthens upon them, they looked more like a tribe in a state of migration than troops engaged in retreat.' Russian shells and Cossack cavalry harassed them in flight, cutting many down, although Scarlett's Heavy Brigade did move forward to give some cover. The only

compensation was that, as in No. 1, the British NCOs spiked the six 12-pounder guns.

After dismantling the two guns in No. 4 redoubt and tumbling their broken parts down the slopes of the Causeway Heights, the Russians abandoned the fortification to concentrate on Nos. 1–3. Fired on by Russian infantry thus established on the Causeway Heights and close to the Kadikoi gorge, where he was dangerously near to the line of fire from the inner defences seeking to hit the Russians, Lucan withdrew his division westwards below Nos. 4 and 5 redoubts. In theory he would then be able to deal with any Russian cavalry attack into the South Valley from the Causeway Heights by charging its flank.

By 8.30am, however, without doubt the outer defences of Balaclava (bearing in mind that Nos. 5 and 6 redoubts were not manned) had fallen. As one eyewitness put it, 'a distressing page for the military history of England' had been completed. The first phase of the Battle of Balaclava was over.

▶ *General François Certain Canrobert. Canrobert became French Commander-in-Chief in the Crimea upon the death of Marshal St. Arnaud in September 1854, whose second-in-command he had been. Canrobert accompanied Lord Raglan when he carried out his reconnaissance of the Crimean coast which resulted in the choice of Calamita Bay for the Allied landings. Never happy in command of the French force, he was to resign the post in favour of General Pélissier. He gave his name to the hill on which No. 1 redoubt was built behind the Causeway Heights and which sustained the first Russian attack during the Battle of Balaclava. In that battle, quickly appreciating the danger to the British lines of communication, he ordered French infantry and cavalry down from the Uplands to assist. (David Paul)*

PHASE 2
THE THIN RED LINE

Before the capture of No. 1 redoubt, and alerted by Lucan's ADC of the enemy's advance, Lord Raglan had taken position on the edge of the Sapoune Ridge overlooking the Plain of Balaclava. Unable to see the true extent of the Russian menace because of the distant undulating ground, he was perturbed that the enemy might be carrying out an elaborate feint. Perhaps Prince Menshikov wanted him to withdraw troops from the siege lines towards Kamara; then the main assault would occur as more Russian troops poured out of Sevastopol to attack the Chersonese Uplands.

Raglan, therefore, with some reluctance ordered the 1st Division (Duke of Cambridge) and 4th Division (Sir George Cathcart) down from the Ridge to the Plain. Cathcart, in particular, was slow to react, having been the unhappy victim in similar circumstances of the false alarm on 21 October. Cambridge, camped closer to Sevastopol,

had further to march. Neither would reach the battlefield before 10.30. By then, three of the four phases of the battle would be over and neither division be in a position to influence the fourth. At the same time that he issued orders to Cambridge and Cathcart, as an insurance, the British commander-in-chief advised Sir Richard England (commander of the 3rd Division) to guard against a surprise foray from Sevastopol.

Independently assessing the threat to the British lines of communication, the French commander-in-chief (following St. Arnaud's death, General Canrobert) sent two brigades from Bosquet's 'Corps of Observation' via the Col into the South Valley. After one had briefly moved towards Kadikoi, it was recalled; and the two French formations took position at the western end of the South Valley under the Chersonese Uplands. Canrobert also ordered eight *Chasseurs d'Afrique* squadrons under General d'Allonville from the Uplands on to the Plain. As he did so, Raglan became alarmed at the exposed situation of Lucan's Cavalry Division. He sent Captain Wetherall to withdraw it even further west 'to the left of the second line of redoubts occupied by the Turks'. Under Wetherall's direction, Lucan therefore took his brigades back under the lee of the Sapoune Ridge beyond No. 6 redoubt.

Meanwhile, Liprandi had been further strengthened by the arrival of Zhaboritski's force, which had advanced on to the Fedioukine Hills. He now had some 25,000 men and 78 guns at his disposal. Of crucial importance for the second phase of the battle were the cavalry units under Ryzhov, which with their artillery support were drawn up across the North Valley – their right flank resting on the Fedioukine Hills, their left on the lower slopes of the Causeway Heights under the captured redoubts. Shortly after 8.30, Liprandi ordered Ryzhov to lead his fourteen hussar squadrons and one Cossack regiment plus another three squadrons from the 53rd Don Cossack Regiment (some 2,300 horsemen) 'against the enemy camp'. The precise meaning of that order was not clear: some officers thought their objective an artillery park near Kadikoi, others the British lines of communication. A direct assault on Balaclava itself, though, was out of the question. Ryzhov had no infantry

▲ *Major-General Sir Colin Campbell. Of humble Scottish background, Sir Colin Campbell had served with distinction during the French and Napoleonic Wars – with Sir John Moore, at Walcheren and in the Peninsula. He later went to the West Indies, China and India. He commanded the Highland Brigade at the Battle of* the Alma and was put in charge of the defences of Balaclava, a post he held on 25 October 1854. Later in the campaign he was to command the 1st Division. After the Crimean War, he became Commander-in-Chief, India, where he suppressed the Indian Mutiny, for which he was created Baron Clyde. (Selby)

'The Thin Red Line'

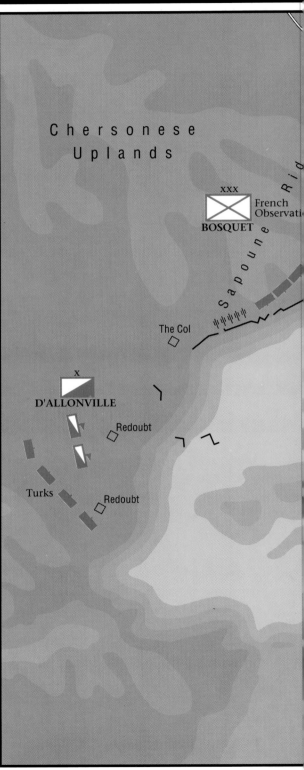

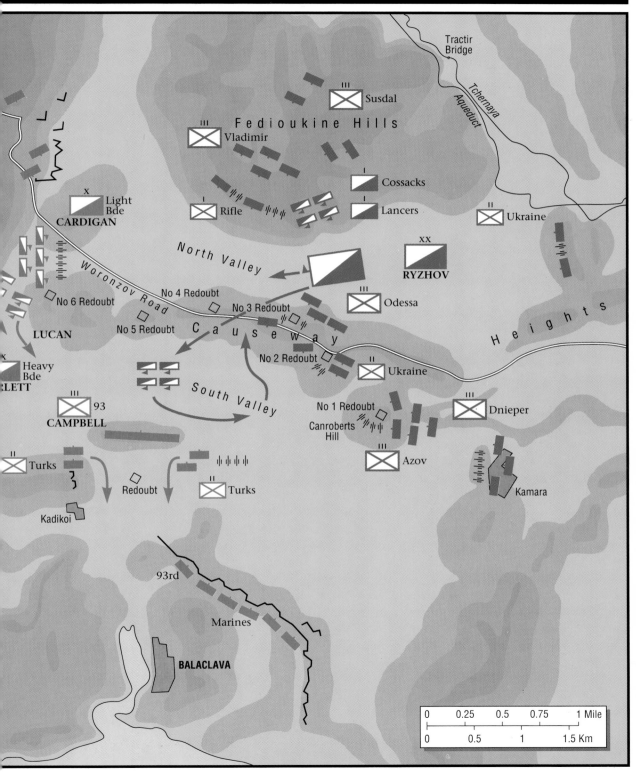

Tractir Bridge

Tchernaya Aqueduct

Susdal

Fedioukine Hills

Vladimir

Cossacks

Lancers

Ukraine

Light Bde
CARDIGAN

Rifle

North Valley

RYZHOV

Woronzov Road

No 4 Redoubt

No 6 Redoubt

No 3 Redoubt

Odessa

LUCAN

No 5 Redoubt

Causeway

Heights

Heavy Bde
RLETT

No 2 Redoubt

Ukraine

South Valley

93

CAMPBELL

No 1 Redoubt

Canroberts Hill

Dnieper

Turks

Redoubt

Turks

Azov

Kamara

Kadikoi

93rd

Marines

BALACLAVA

| 0 | 0.25 | 0.5 | 0.75 | 1 Mile |
| 0 | 0.5 | 1 | 1.5 Km | |

support; and he was extremely worried about possible dug-in infantry in his path. As events were to prove, this fear of infantry fire was well-founded.

As Ryzhov rode westwards along the North Valley, Campbell finalized the defences around Kadikoi. The two companies of the 93rd that had been in Balaclava had now joined the other six on the knoll north of the village, which would later be named 'Sutherland Hillock'. So 550 Sutherland Highlanders were drawn up on the crest together with some forty men on detached duty in Balaclava brought up to swell their numbers by two enterprising Guards officers. About 100 invalids under the command of Colonel Daveney, which had been on their way to Balaclava from the divisional camps in front of Sevastopol, were also pressed into service and took post to the left of the 93rd. Campbell already had one Turkish battalion under command and, rallying many of those fleeing from the redoubts, he formed a second *ad hoc* battalion. He then deployed one Turkish battalion on the right and one on the left of his central British force. Barker's six field guns were nearby, and two of the longer-range guns of the inner defences could also be called upon for support. Campbell's infantry comprised in total some 700 British and 1,000 Turks. On them rested control of the gorge leading directly into Balaclava.

Before the Russian cavalry appeared, shells from the Causeway Heights wounded two Highlanders, and Campbell withdrew his British troops to the reverse slope of the knoll. They were thus out of sight of the Russian cavalry, even if they were to breast the Causeway Heights to enter the South Valley.

Meanwhile, riding along the North Valley, Ryzhov detached four squadrons of hussars across the Causeway Heights east of No. 4 redoubt towards Kadikoi. When they were about 1,000 yards from the village, Campbell ordered the 93rd and the other British soldiers back to the top of the rise, where 'the thin red line' (as it was to become known to posterity) formed two ranks instead of the more traditional square in the face of cavalry. However, they found their flanks dangerously exposed – confused by the sudden appearance of the enemy riding down on them in

apparent strength and seeing the withdrawal of the British infantry from the crest of the knoll under fire, many of the Turks had once more panicked and fled towards Balaclava. The few that stayed behind were rallied by Campbell, who sternly addressed his small force as he rode down the line: 'Remember there is no retreat from here, men! You must die where you stand!'

Approaching from roughly north–north–east and already subjected to heavy fire from British gunners (principally grape fired by Barker's battery), on seeing the Highlanders rise suddenly and dramatically from the high ground immediately in front of them, the Russians faltered. They may well have suspected an ambush, believing that more troops were about to engulf them. Their hesitation prompted the Highlanders to edge forward yelling in anticipation of a charge. Campbell knew better than to give up his vantage point. 'Ninety-third! Ninety-third! Damn all that eagerness!' he roared to restrain them. As he did so, although at extreme range, the Highlanders loosed off a fierce volley. No enemy fell from the saddle, but clearly men and horses were wounded, and the Russians wheeled left. In doing this, they threatened Campbell's weak right flank. Recognizing the danger, he reformed to pour a second volley into the Russians. They then turned further to the left away from Kadikoi and began to retire in disorder. Distracted momentarily from the plight of their vanquished foe, some of the defenders beheld an amusing episode. Near Kadikoi, one of the Turks, who had taken to his heels, was being soundly beaten and verbally abused by the formidable and angry wife of a soldier. In the words of the Crimean War writer, A. W. Kinglake, 'the men of the 93rd were able to witness this incident. It mightily pleased them.'

So did the retreat of the Russians. Whatever the four squadrons had intended – capture of the mythical artillery park, interference with the supply lines or seizure of Kadikoi – they had clearly and humiliatingly failed, defeated by a disparate collection of able-bodied infantry, invalids and a few Turks, closely supported by a single field battery. The inner defences of Balaclava had held. Shortly after 9am, the second phase of the battle was over. This time, the British had won.

PHASE 3
CHARGE OF THE HEAVY BRIGADE

Watching the advance of the Russian cavalry towards Kadikoi from his vantage point above the battlefield, Lord Raglan saw the Turks on Campbell's flanks begin to waver. He therefore sent a message to Lord Lucan at the Cavalry Division's new position under the Sapoune Ridge, urging him to give Campbell active support. Lucan in turn ordered Scarlett to take eight squadrons of the Heavy Brigade to Kadikoi. Unknown to either officer, Scarlett was about to fight his first-ever battle at the age of 55. In the process, he would cover himself and his brigade in glory.

The Russian Advance

Still advancing westwards along the North Valley, after detaching the four hussar squadrons and Cossacks towards Kadikoi, Ryzhov came under fire from Allied batteries firing down on him from the Sapoune Ridge. However, just short of No. 5 redoubt, he wheeled his enormous body of cavalry left into South Valley aiming towards Kadikoi from due north. According to one Russian source 'like Murat' (Napoleon's dashing cavalry leader), Ryzhov personally led the advance, not deigning even to draw his sword. Behind him the Ingerman-land Regiment formed the first line in open order; in the second line rode the Kiev Regiment in column of attack. Cossacks covered the flanks. In reserve was another Cossack regiment, with the additional Composite Uhlan Regiment remaining under Liprandi's direct control.

Trotting over the Causeway Heights, Ryzhov saw Scarlett moving across his front. Then the Heavy Brigade turned to meet him. When a little under 500 yards from his enemy, as he rode down the slope, Ryzhov became aware that the British were preparing to attack. Meanwhile, Liprandi, either sensing danger or, more likely, recognizing an opportunity to eliminate an inferior enemy

force, ordered the reserve Cossacks into battle. Galloping hard and keeping up 'their everlasting screaming', they followed their own separate line of advance some 200 yards to the left of Ryzhov, where they would exert no real influence on the conflict. Already, British artillery in the Kadikoi area was finding its mark in the Russian ranks.

As it did so, Scarlett was deploying his small force to attack. Then, inexplicably, Ryzhov halted his main body, a mere 100 yards from the Heavy Brigade. Later he claimed that he had needed to reorganize his two hussar regiments side by side in the face of the extended line that Scarlett was forming. Perhaps so. However, he undoubtedly gave Scarlett the opportunity to charge a superior force while it remained stationary.

The Heavy Brigade Deploys

The Heavy Brigade commander had had difficult terrain to negotiate after leaving his position beneath the Sapoune Ridge to move eastwards. Apart from the broken nature of the lower slopes of the Causeway Heights over which the squadrons must move, there were two major obstacles. Just south of No. 6 redoubt lay an extensive, fenced vineyard (in some sources 'plantation') around which Scarlett must pass. This would clearly delay his advance. East of that area lay the Light Brigade camp, which had been abandoned in haste earlier in the morning. There, tents were still standing, while picket ropes and a few tethered sick animals remained. It was no place to fight a battle, let alone one where the cavalry had to pick its way uphill against larger numbers.

Scarlett had advanced with his squadrons in two columns parallel to the Causeway Heights and eighty yards away. On the right, furthest from the Causeway, one squadron of the Inniskilling Dragoons led, followed by both squadrons of the

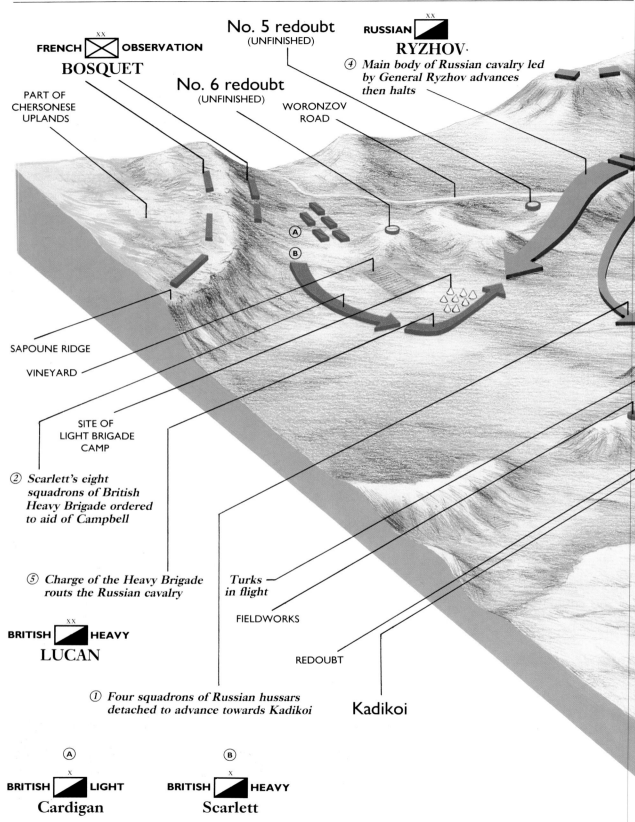

FRENCH ⊠ **OBSERVATION**
XX
BOSQUET

No. 5 redoubt
(UNFINISHED)

RUSSIAN ◨
XX
RYZHOV·

④ *Main body of Russian cavalry led by General Ryzhov advances then halts*

No. 6 redoubt
(UNFINISHED)

PART OF
CHERSONESE
UPLANDS

WORONZOV
ROAD

Ⓐ

Ⓑ

SAPOUNE RIDGE

VINEYARD

SITE OF
LIGHT BRIGADE
CAMP

② *Scarlett's eight squadrons of British Heavy Brigade ordered to aid of Campbell*

⑤ *Charge of the Heavy Brigade routs the Russian cavalry*

Turks
in flight

FIELDWORKS

BRITISH ◨ **HEAVY**
XX
LUCAN

REDOUBT

① *Four squadrons of Russian hussars detached to advance towards Kadikoi*

Kadikoi

Ⓐ
BRITISH ◨ **LIGHT**
X
Cardigan

Ⓑ
BRITISH ◨ **HEAVY**
X
Scarlett

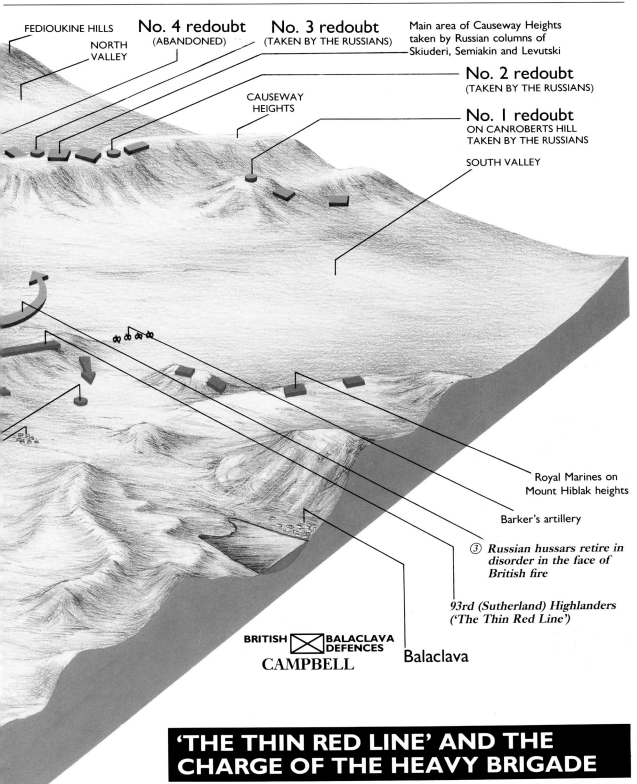

FEDIOUKINE HILLS

NORTH VALLEY

No. 4 redoubt (ABANDONED)

No. 3 redoubt (TAKEN BY THE RUSSIANS)

Main area of Causeway Heights taken by Russian columns of Skiuderi, Semiakin and Levutski

No. 2 redoubt (TAKEN BY THE RUSSIANS)

CAUSEWAY HEIGHTS

No. 1 redoubt ON CANROBERTS HILL TAKEN BY THE RUSSIANS

SOUTH VALLEY

Royal Marines on Mount Hiblak heights

Barker's artillery

③ *Russian hussars retire in disorder in the face of British fire*

93rd (Sutherland) Highlanders ('The Thin Red Line')

BRITISH ⊠ BALACLAVA DEFENCES

CAMPBELL

Balaclava

'THE THIN RED LINE' AND THE CHARGE OF THE HEAVY BRIGADE

8.45 to 9.30am, 25 October 1854: Phases 2 and 3 of the Battle of Balaclava.

5th Dragoon Guards. The second Inniskilling squadron headed the left-hand column in front of the Scots Greys. The two squadrons of the 4th Dragoon Guards were further behind both columns. Scarlett and his ADC, Lieutenant Alexander Elliot, rode on the left of the left-hand column. They had been just skirting the Light Brigade camp when Elliot spotted the tips of lances above the Causeway Heights. According to some later reports, being short-sighted, Scarlett had thought these fuzzy shapes represented thistles, not enemy weapons; nevertheless, he soon recovered his poise. No longer was he bent on reaching Kadikoi. A more potent danger had appeared on his flank.

Determined to attack the enemy, Scarlett ordered 'left wheel into line!' The left-hand column did, but as the Scots Greys were scarcely clear of the vineyard, Scarlett further ordered the squadrons to 'take ground to the right'. This would certainly put them east of the vineyard but cause them to advance through the disorder of the partially-struck Light Brigade camp. Evidently Scarlett hoped that all six of his squadrons would attack by forming two extended lines, one behind the other. Warfare in its execution is seldom perfect. The right column had become divided on the march: the Inniskilling squadron in the van was well in advance of the 5th Dragoons on the right. So, when the order to wheel into line was given, the 5th Dragoons actually drew up slightly to the left rear of the Scots Greys. But the Inniskilling were far to the right in a very exposed position. The whole manoeuvre had been further complicated because the right-hand column had been marching by threes, the left-hand in open column. The actual charge would therefore take time to organize. And Scarlett would not be hurried. Perhaps this is what puzzled Ryzhov. As Raglan had earlier feared a ruse to allow a major attack out of Sevastopol, and the Russian hussars approaching Kadikoi suspected an ambush, Scarlett might be leading Ryzhov into a trap. Otherwise, why would he show so little alarm? Hence the bewildered Russians came to a halt. And Scarlett unhurriedly dressed his ranks.

Unknown to him, Raglan had alerted Lucan to the strength of the threat. As Scarlett's officers were dressing their men with parade-ground precision, the 4th Dragoons were riding to help them. So, too, was the impatient Lucan. Galloping up as Scarlett wheeled his men into line for the second time, after moving to the right, he urged him to attack at once. With their backs to the enemy, however, officers calmly brought the squadrons into line. The first line had the two squadrons of Scots Greys on the left, the Inniskillings squadron on the right. The second line effectively had only the 5th Dragoons to the left rear of the Scots Greys: the other Inniskilling squadron remained too far to the right to support anybody. It was as the dressing was in progress that the Russian trumpets sounded and Ryzhov's force came to a halt. Shortly afterwards, Russian horsemen were seen pushing out to the left and right fronts of the main body, giving the whole force something of a crab-like appearance, with claws ready to grasp an attacker.

Possibly aware of the danger to Scarlett if the enemy completed this movement before he charged, Lucan testily ordered the divisional trumpeter to sound the charge. In vain. If the squadrons heard him, they paid more attention to their own officers. Then at last the Heavy Brigade was ready. Scarlett with Elliot, his own trumpeter and orderly formed a tiny group ten yards in front of the first line. So eager were the Inniskillings in the first line to be away that Scarlett had to restrain them with his outstretched sword. They, fortunately, were well clear of the Light Brigade camp with an unrestricted view of the enemy and an unimpeded path in front. Not so the Scots Greys on their left. Finally, the front line did go forward; but Scarlett soon found himself leading just three squadrons against almost 2,000 enemy cavalry. 'Scarlett's 300', as they were later called, followed the drill book. First came the order, 'the line will advance at a walk', then the trumpet successively sounded 'trot', 'gallop' and 'charge'. Like Lucan, recognizing the absolute need to hit the enemy while he was still reforming and before he was himself attacked, Scarlett told his trumpeter to sound 'charge' almost as soon as the squadrons began to advance. But the Scots Greys, in particular, could not obey. The Light Brigade camp was proving a most difficult area to negotiate.

Anxious not to dawdle, Scarlett half-turned in his saddle to urge the Scots Greys forward more quickly. They did pick up speed gradually, but when Scarlett and his small party drove into the Russian front, they were still fifty yards ahead of the nearest British horsemen.

The Charge

To the spectators on the Sapoune Ridge, the scene was pure theatre. Elliot in his cocked hat rode beside Scarlett, who wore a blue frocked coat and burnished helmet rather than a general's head-dress. Slightly behind them rode a solitary trumpeter and Scarlett's massive orderly Shegog. Together these four spurred ahead of the following squadrons. As the Scots Greys and Inniskillings sought to catch their brigade commander, he vanished into the enemy mass. He did so close to a Russian officer who, like him, had taken post in advance of his men. Elliot's sword transfixed the

Russian, but the impetus of the charge swung his body round as Elliot struggled to pull the sword out before being engulfed.

When the Scots Greys and Inniskillings bore down on the Russians, they met ragged, but effective, carbine fire. One of the first casualties was Lieutenant-Colonel Henry Griffith, commanding the Scots Greys, who was hit in the head. Major George Clarke, leading the right squadron of the Regiment, was luckier: he lost his bearskin, as his excited horse galloped forward, so he entered the Russian ranks bare-headed. The Inniskillings led by Lieutenant-Colonel Dalrymple White were the first to reach the Russians after Scarlett's party, cheering madly as they did so. The Scots Greys, however, were not far behind, uttering a sort of fierce low moan.

Soon they were all fighting for their lives – 300 against 2,000. The Russians, mostly wearing heavy grey greatcoats and protective shakos, were so closely packed that the British found it difficult to

▶ *Brigadier-General The Honourable James Yorke Scarlett. Originally entering the Army in 1818, Scarlett had commanded the 5th Dragoon Guards (1840–54) without seeing active service. Appointed to command the Heavy Brigade with Lord Raglan's Expeditionary Force, he distinguished himself at the Battle of Balaclava. Later in the campaign, he commanded the Cavalry Division and, after the war, became Adjutant-General at the Horse Guards. (Selby)*

▲ *Colonel William Ferguson Beatson. An experienced officer with irregular cavalry, Beatson had served with distinction under Sir George de Lacy Evans (commander of the 2nd Division in the Crimea) in Spain during the Carlist Wars and also with the Nizam of Hyderabad in India. The British government had hoped that he would organize*

Turkish irregular cavalry in support of the British troops with Lord Raglan. When this plan failed to materialize, General Scarlett used Beatson as an additional ADC. He was therefore influential in training the Heavy Brigade, but did not charge with it on 25 October 1854. He watched the Battle of Balaclava from the Sapoune Ridge. (David Paul)

wield their swords to effect. When they did so, the points rarely penetrated the thick Russian clothing. Only a few Russians were wearing a distinctive pale blue pelisse or hussar jacket. The British had red uniforms and helmets (with the exception of the Scots Greys, who wore bearskins). They did not wear shoulder scales, the restricting throat stocks or gauntlets. They were, therefore, in some respects more vulnerable than the light cavalry (hussars and lancers) who opposed them. The spectacle of small groups of red coats or desperate, isolated individuals hacking their way through the grey mass below them was both awesome and inspiring to the watchers high above the field. There, 1½ miles away on the Sapoune Ridge, the roars of men, neighs of horses and clash of steel on steel drifted on the breeze adding to the atmosphere of battle. But these indistinct noises could not convey the terror, bravery and sheer exhaustion being experienced amid that heaving throng.

Jabbing, slicing and cleaving his way forward, Scarlett sustained blows to the head that severely dented his helmet without scratching him, and elsewhere he suffered five wounds to his body. Here was a commander who led by example. His ADC (Elliot) was more seriously injured. At one point surrounded with little hope of survival, he was saved by his maddened charger's lashing hooves. In all, Elliot sustained fourteen sabre cuts, one of which slashed his face extensively so that several stitches had later to be inserted. Another blow split his cocked hat and yet another temporarily knocked him out. He stayed in the saddle, however, and lived. The bare-headed Clarke predictably received a deep cut in his skull. Fortunately, it was at the rear, and the blood flowed freely down his neck unknown to him in the heat of conflict as he fought his way forward. Dalrymple White found himself fighting alone, suffered a blow which split his helmet in two and similarly was unaware of what had happened.

Some of the 300 actually emerged, having blasted their way right through the Russians, to face Cossack reserves drawn up behind the main body. As they did so the claws thrust out in front of the enemy force began to close behind them. A Light Brigade officer looking on gasped: 'They are surrounded, and must be annihilated. One can hardly breathe!' The truth was that, in that dreadful mêlée, this actually did apply to many a struggling man. Help seemed so far away. Realizing that unless his men rallied they were doomed, the adjutant of the Scots Greys bellowed above the din: 'Rally the Greys . . . Rally the Greys!' Bravely he backed down the hill, ordering his men to face

▼ *Officer, 4th (Royal Irish) Dragoon Guards. Riding east of the prominent vineyard in the South Valley and led by Lieutenant-Colonel Edward Hodge, the 4th Dragoons drove through the main body of Russian cavalry from left to right as it halted on the southern slopes of the Causeway Heights to receive the charge of the Heavy Brigade.*

▼*Charge of the Heavy Brigade. In the foreground is the imperfectly struck Light Brigade camp, through which some of the squadrons had to pick their way. This inaccurate reconstruction of events* shows the first line of Inniskillings and Scots Greys (nearer), with the 5th Dragoons in close support. The second Inniskilling squadron is shown in the distance simultaneously asaulting the enemy left, while the 4th Dragoons appear just to the right of the scene. The 93rd on its knoll is shown in the middle distance, Kadikoi on the right and Balaclava in the background. The artist also depicts local Tartars plundering the Light Brigade camp during the attack. (Sandhurst)

him and reform – an incredible demand. Yet, still in that milling throng, many did manage to close on one another and the squadrons did achieve some sort of order. Without that, a lot more must have perished.

In the meantime, the other three squadrons near to Scarlett as he closed on Kadikoi had attacked after the first line. The 5th Dragoons, who formed up in extended line slightly to the left rear of the Scots Greys, were seriously hampered by the Light Brigade camp, and some riders were unseated as their horses stumbled over picket ropes. Clearing these obstructions the two squadrons hit the forward part of the Russian right wing

Charge of the Heavy Brigade

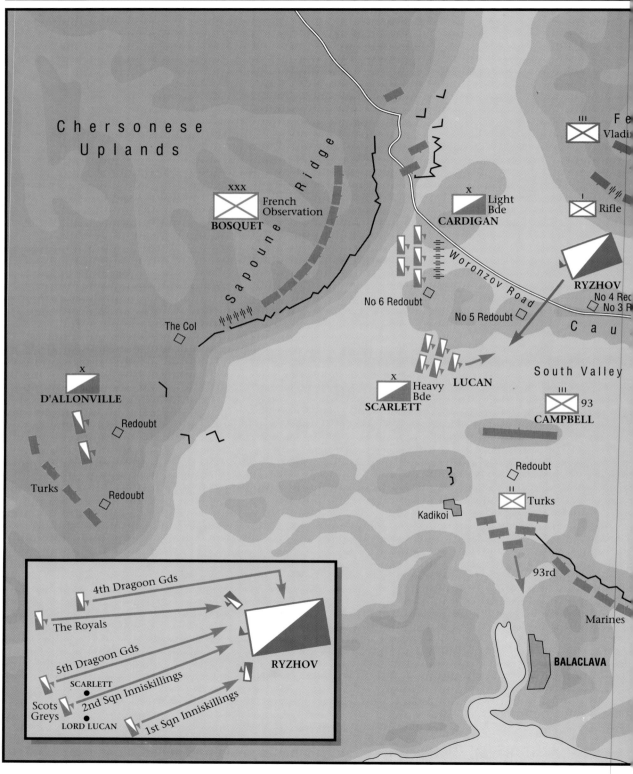

Chersonese Uplands

Sapoune Ridge

French Observation

XXX
BOSQUET

The Col

Redoubt

x
D'ALLONVILLE

Turks

Redoubt

Woronzov Road

x
CARDIGAN
Light Bde

No 6 Redoubt

No 5 Redoubt

III
Vladi
Fe

I
Rifle

RYZHOV
No 4 Red
No 3 R

C a u

x
SCARLETT
Heavy Bde

LUCAN

South Valley

III
CAMPBELL
93

Redoubt

II
Turks

Kadikoi

93rd

Marines

BALACLAVA

4th Dragoon Gds

The Royals

5th Dragoon Gds

SCARLETT

Scots Greys

2nd Sqn Inniskillings

LORD LUCAN

1st Sqn Inniskillings

RYZHOV

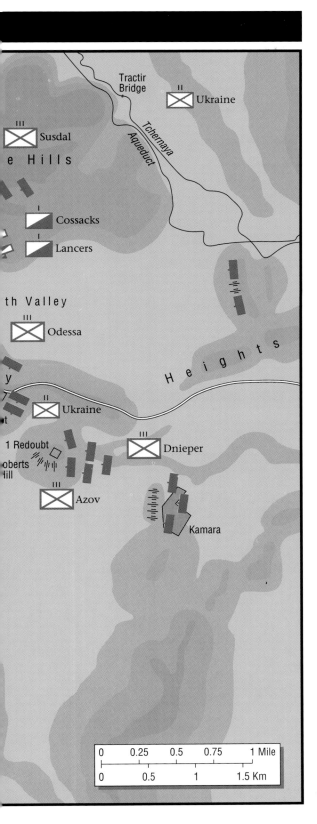

as the 'claw' wheeled and many of the troopers had their backs to the British dragoons. Subjected to some carbine fire, nevertheless the 5th Dragoons struck the enemy just as the Scots Greys were being forced back in the centre. Their arrival was therefore most opportune. Away to the right, in its detached position, the other Inniskilling squadron attacked the Russian left. Because of its relatively-advanced situation on the march to Kadikoi, under Major Charles Shute this squadron approached the enemy from an oblique angle. With no impediments in their path, the cavalrymen quickly picked up speed, and their advance was helped by thick herbage underfoot, which effectively muffled the hooves. Incredibly, like the 5th Dragoons on the far left of the attack, Shute's force struck the Russian left wing ('claw' extension) as it was turning inwards. Driving rapidly into the mass, the dragoons seemed to carry the Russians back uphill with them. The unexpected nature and fury of their assault had caught the enemy completely by surprise. One Inniskilling officer carried a dead Russian across his saddle into the close-packed ranks, unable to throw the corpse off for lack of room.

Arriving in the area of the vineyard shortly after the first six squadrons, the 4th Dragoons had seen Scarlett's 300 quickly and alarmingly vanish into the massed grey files. Skirting the eastern fence of the vineyard and picking their way through the western part of the Light Brigade camp, the two squadrons under Lieutenant-Colonel Edward Hodge advanced parallel to Scarlett's line of attack to the west of the Russians, before turning almost at right-angles to charge the enemy right flank. Hacking their way forward, they drove straight through to come out on the enemy's eastern (left) flank. Hodge emerged about the same time as, and close to, Scatlett, who had fought in a half circle to his right and also emerged half way along the enemy left flank.

The two squadrons of The Royals that had been left behind with the Light Brigade followed their commanding officer (Lieutenant-Colonel John Yorke), who acted on his own initiative without receiving orders. Advancing in the wake of the rest of the Heavy Brigade, The Royals had passed the vineyard just as the Scots Greys

▲ *Another portrayal of Brigadier-General Scarlett's charge, showing the Scots Greys (in bearskins), with The Royals too close behind them. Note the Russian officer in the centre discharging his pistol, but the men behind him still with their swords at the slope. (Sandhurst)*

▼ *This contemporary print attempts to convey more of the confusion, death and smoke on the battlefield. (David Paul)*

appeared to be in dire trouble prior to their adjutant's command to rally and as the 4th Dragoons were preparing to launch their flank attack. A voice called: 'By God, the Greys are cut off! Gallop! Gallop!' The Royals cheered and surged forward quickly, with the result that they did not put in a coordinated attack on the enemy right. But their appearance served further to confuse the Russians, who were now being attacked from a fourth direction. The Royals only exchanged 'a few sabre-cuts' with the enemy, incurring minor casualties, before Yorke recalled them to reform. Prior to that order, however, Troop Sergeant Norris had suffered a bizarre experience. Delayed by clutter in the Light Brigade camp, he had galloped hard to catch the others, but was cornered by four Russians. Reacting vigorously, he killed one and drove off the other three.

As Scarlett and Hodge came out of the enemy left, the Russians were beginning to break. Afraid that his men would pursue them too far and be exposed to decimating artillery fire or counter-attack, Hodge ordered the nearest trumpeter to sound the rally. It was only just in time. The Dragoons had already come under fire from batteries across the North Valley on the Fediou-kine Hills. As the enemy broke, Barker's battery near Kadikoi, Maude's battery with the Light Brigade and three Turkish guns in a defence-work close to the Col of Balaclava opened fire on them. In desperation, Liprandi sent forward his reserve lancers from the Composite Uhlan Regiment. When case-shot began to hit them, he reversed the order. It was all over. Russian sources later admitted to being 'crushed'.

The whole action from the time that Scarlett started his charge to the enemy retreat took a mere eight minutes. It cost the Heavy Brigade 78 casualties; the Russians suffered 270, including Major-General Khaletski wounded. The threat to Kadikoi had again been stemmed. The inner defences of Balaclava remained intact.

A watching French general declared: 'The victory of the Heavy Brigade was the most glorious thing I ever saw.' Edward Hamley similarly observed: 'All those, who had the good fortune to look down from the Heights on this brilliant spectacle, had a vivid recollection of it.' Away to the east, the cheers of the 93rd carried on the wind, and Campbell rode up to offer his personal congratulations. Doffing his hat, he cried: 'Greys! Gallant Greys! I am sixty-one years old, and if I were young again I should be proud to be in your ranks.' To Scarlett, Raglan sent a short, but heartfelt, message: 'Well done!'

Well done, indeed. But what of the Light Brigade, whose 700 men had watched the engagement idly from afar? A flank attack by them might well have cleared the enemy cavalry right off the battlefield and back across the Tchernaya. Unknown to them at the time, it would also have prevented the military holocaust that lay in store for them.

500 yards to the west, the Light Brigade was drawn up in two lines, to one embittered cavalryman as 'spectators'. Cardigan, despite pleas from his officers, would not move. Yet, according to many, he rode restlessly up and down the line muttering: 'Damn those Heavies, they have the laugh of us this day.' Vicomte de Noe, an experienced French observer, believed that the retreating Russians could have been 'annihilated' if Cardigan had charged their flank. 'This was the occasion', he concluded, when 'there should have been exercised the initiative of the cavalry general.' Cardigan blamed his inactivity upon his hated brother-in-law. He later explained: 'I had been ordered into position by the Earl of Lucan, my superior officer, with orders on no account to leave it, and to defend it against any attack of Russians.' He added laconically: 'They did not, however, approach the position.' In his mind, therefore, his lack of action was both logical and excusable. His orders had not permitted him any latitude. As de Noe added, 'Later in the day it was made apparent that bravery is no sufficient substitute for initiative.'

Cardigan's shortcomings, which could have turned a local victory into a decisive rout, should not obscure the magnitude of Scarlett's achievement. The third phase of the Battle of Balaclava, like the second, had gone in favour of the British. It was still only 9.30, and the spectacular, bloody and unnecessary slaughter of the fourth phase was yet to come.

▼ *Trooper, 11th (Prince Albert's Own) Hussars. Led by Lieutenant-Colonel John Douglas, the 11th Hussars formed the second line during the Charge of the Light Brigade. For twelve years (1836–47), Lord Cardigan had commanded the regiment.*

PHASE 4
CHARGE OF THE LIGHT BRIGADE

Immortalized by Tennyson's striking poem, the fourth and last phase of the battle took place in the North Valley between 11.00 and 11.20. For many people, this action alone represents 'The Battle of Balaclava'. The previous three actions, even if they are acknowledged, pale into insignificance. The Charge of the Light Brigade has overshadowed all else in memory.

Repulsed by Scarlett's Heavy Brigade, Ryzhov's cavalry reformed at the eastern end of the North Valley with Zhaboritski's infantry and artillery sheltering them from the Fedioukine Hills, and Liprandi's other troops (infantry, artillery and cavalry) deployed on high ground along the Causeway Heights between No. 3 redoubt and Kamara. In front of Ryzhov's squadrons were eight guns (though British sources claim twelve) of the 3rd Don Cossack Field Battery drawn up across the floor of the Valley. Colonel V. M. Yeropkin's Composite Uhlan Regiment acted as a mobile link between the Causeway Heights and the Fedioukine Hills. Ninety minutes after the close of the Heavy Brigade action, Ryzhov trotted down to speak to Prince Obolenski, commander of the Don Battery. Suddenly gunners drew the attention of the officers to a distant cloud of dust. It seemed to be creeping closer down the Valley. In amazement, Ryzhov realized that the British cavalry were mounting an attack. The Don Battery prepared to open fire once the riders came within range.

The long delay before the British followed up Scarlett's success against the shaken Russians occurred through a series of unfortunate circumstances. Despite repeated messages from Raglan stressing urgency, the infantry divisions of the Duke of Cambridge and Sir George Cathcart took an inordinate time to reach the Plain of Balaclava. Cambridge descended directly into the North Valley close to the Woronzov Road, while Cathcart moved along the Ridge via the Col to the South

Valley. Each division covered a distance of between five and six miles. Although at about 10.30 they did arrive on the Plain, their subsequent advance on the Causeway Heights had yet to be coordinated. Raglan, as his earlier orders suggested, wanted to use both divisions to recover ground lost on the Causeway Heights. Initially, he expected them to attack the Russians in No. 3 redoubt. The ideal time to have done so would have been shortly after the hussars and Cossacks routed by Scarlett streamed over the Heights. Now a more organized enemy awaited them.

Orders

Impatience at the tardy passage of his infantry prompted Raglan to use cavalry to unsettle the Russians. He therefore dispatched an order to Lucan shortly after 10.15: 'Cavalry to advance and take advantage of any opportunity to recover the Heights. They will be supported by the infantry which have been ordered to advance on two fronts.' There were only the Causeway 'Heights' to 'recover'; and the cavalry's role was therefore quite clear – or should have been – to Lucan. 'On two fronts' might have meant Campbell advancing from Kadikoi in cooperation with the 1st and 4th Divisions. In fact, the plan was for Cambridge and Cathcart to approach the captured redoubts on the Causeway Heights from the North and South valleys respectively. Receiving Raglan's order, Lucan immediately moved the Light Brigade into the North Valley, keeping the Heavy Brigade close to No. 6 redoubt in the South Valley, Justifiably, he did not intend to launch any attack until the British infantry arrived, and certainly not against prepared enemy positions. Whatever the later argument about the objective of the Light Brigade in its charge, at this stage there could have been no doubt about Lord Raglan's intention: recapture of the redoubts.

Much of the Causeway Heights, and indeed the ground in the North Valley, was obscured by undulating land from Lucan, as he waited with his staff between the two brigades on the lower slopes of the Causeway Heights. He could not see, as Raglan and his staff could, that Russian artillerymen with horses and lassoes were preparing to take away the captured guns from Nos. 1–3 redoubts. Conscious that the capture of guns was frequently used to claim victory, Raglan was doubly anxious that the Russians should not succeed in this manoeuvre. Exasperated by Lucan's inactivity, he dictated another order – the one that thereafter would be the subject of bitter and protracted debate. 'Lord Raglan wishes the cavalry to advance rapidly to the front, and try to prevent the enemy carrying away the guns. Troop of horse-artillery may accompany. French cavalry is on your left.'

Fatally, this order was given to the volatile Captain Edward Nolan to deliver to Lucan. Speed was of the essence; and Nolan was a fine horseman, who had served in the Austrian Army and had written books about cavalry tactics. He would make haste, as he did, down the 700-feet escarpment. Unfortunately, Nolan was known to be highly critical of the cavalry's performance so far in the Crimea and, perhaps more pointedly, of Lucan's personal leadership. Later Lucan maintained that he read this message with 'consideration' bordering on 'consternation'. From where he sat, he could see 'neither enemy nor guns'. Lucan asked Nolan for clarification. Nolan, possibly excited by his contempt for Lucan and aching to see the cavalry in action, replied: 'Lord Raglan's orders are, that the cavalry should attack immediately.' Reputedly, Lucan retorted sharply: 'Attack, sir! Attack what? What guns, sir?' Nolan's response, verging on insubordination, was to throw back his head and stretch his arm forward to say: 'There, my lord, is your enemy; there are your guns.' Lucan fumed that he did so in a 'most disrespectful but significant manner'. Sadly, Lucan's pride barred him from questioning Nolan further. Yet, Nolan should not have needed to be more exact. This and the previous order had to be read in conjunction with one another. However,

Lucan chose to attack the Don Battery at the eastern end of the North Valley, not seek 'to recover' the guns on the Causeway Heights.

Trotting over to Cardigan, who sat astride his chestnut thoroughbred Ronald in front of the 13th Light Dragoons, Lucan issued orders to this effect. The antipathy between the two men prevented any prolonged or rational discussion. Cardigan saluted with his drawn sword in acknowledgement of the order: 'Certainly, sir; but allow me to point out to you that the Russians have a battery in the valley in our front, and batteries and riflemen on each flank.' Unhelpfully, his superior officer agreed: 'I know it, but Lord Raglan will have it. We have no choice but to obey.' The die was cast for one of the bloodiest, most glorious and senseless engagements in British military history. If, as mythology claims, Cardigan muttered as he turned away, 'Here goes the last of the Brudenells,' his pessimism appeared justified.

Lucan ordered the 11th Hussars to drop back from the front line to narrow the attacking front, before Cardigan gave the fateful order: 'The brigade will advance!' As he did so, he might well have had in mind Lucan's final warning to 'advance very steadily and quietly'. There were, after all, 1¼ miles to go before the enemy guns. Horses and riders should not arrive too exhausted by a prolonged gallop to fight effectively. Harassed by shot, shell and bullet from three sides, the tendency would be to speed up. Valuable tight formation must not be sacrificed.

'Into the Valley of Death'

Cardigan rode ten yards in front of the first line and five ahead of his staff officers, Lieutenants Maxse and Wombwell. In the uniform of his old regiment, the 11th Hussars, his gold-laced pelisse worn like a coat rather than thrown over his shoulder, Cardigan sat erect in the saddle, his sword at the slope. After the ensuing action, Raglan would dub him 'brave as a lion'. Behind Cardigan, as he set off down the North Valley at 11am on 25 October 1854, the Light Brigade advanced in three lines. The first had on the right the 13th Light Dragoons (Captain John Oldham) and on the left the 17th Lancers (Captain William

Morris); only the 11th Hussars (Lieutenant-Colonel John Douglas) comprised the second line behind the 17th; and the third line had the 4th Light Dragoons (Lieutenant-Colonel Lord George Paget) to the left, 8th Hussars (Lieutenant-Colonel Frederick Shewell) to the right, less one troop at Army Headquarters on the Chersonese Uplands. Each of the regiments rode in extended line, two deep.

The Light Brigade was not alone. Lucan saw the attack as a divisional action. He rode with his staff between the two brigades. Behind him, the Scots Greys on the left and The Royals on the right formed the first line of the Heavy Brigade; the Iniskilling Dragoons were (like the 11th Hussars for the Light Brigade) the entire second line; in the third, the 4th Dragoon Guards rode on the left, the 5th on the right. Awareness that the Heavy Brigade would not move so quickly nor so easily was another consideration behind Lucan's

▶ *Major-General The Earl of Cardigan. Known for his domineering manner and fierce temper, James Thomas Brudenell, Earl of Cardigan, did not enter the Army until aged 27. However, taking advantage of the purchase system, within eight years he had gained command of the 15th Hussars, from which he was removed after little more than a year for unreasonable behaviour. His purchase of command of the 11th Light Dragoons (later renamed Hussars) in 1836 caused a furore. But the purchase stood, and he remained in command until 1847. Appointed to command the Light Brigade in the Crimea, he applied the strict discipline to which he was used. If his judgement and good sense may be questioned, his courage (not least during the celebrated charge on 25 October 1854) was never in doubt. (David Paul)*

caution to Cardigan against riding too fast.

Unknown to the British, as soon as the advance commenced, orders were issued to the Odessa Regiment and accompanying field artillery to withdraw from the area of No. 3 redoubt. In terms of firepower this would have little effect. Cardigan's men must still, as Lord Tennyson so graphically explained, face cannon to right, left and front only too ready to volley and thunder.

Despite Lucan's call for restraint, however, Cardigan quickly began to trot, acutely aware of the dangers that lay ahead. Behind him, the regiments kept pace. Significantly, there was one outsider among them. Captain Nolan was riding with his friend Morris of the 17th Lancers. Quite suddenly, and quite extraordinarily, after the Brigade had progressed a hundred yards, he surged forward, galloped ahead of Cardigan, crossing his front from left to right. Turning in his saddle, Nolan shouted and waved his sword aloft. Close observers believed that the line that he was taking would have carried him to No. 3 redoubt and the first of the guns still in Russian possession. He might, indeed, have realized that Cardigan was attacking the wrong guns, not advancing towards those on the Causeway Heights. But, at the moment that he began to shout a possible warning, a shell splinter pierced his chest. His sword dropped dramatically to the ground, though the lifeless arm remained aloft. As the reins lost the rider's grip, his terrified horse plunged back through the advancing 17th Lancers, the 'corpse' uttering an 'unearthly' shriek before it toppled to earth.

Behind Cardigan, the Heavy Brigade was also under way. However, it inevitably lost ground as the Light Brigade increased speed. A dangerous gap opened between the two brigades, and Lucan had a difficult choice to make. Press on or halt? For some distance, he and his staff tried to keep the Light Brigade in sight – an impossible task as the smoke and dust ahead thickened. The riders gradually disappeared from view. Coming abreast of No. 4 redoubt, Captain Charteris fell dead at Lucan's side, and his other two ADCs were either unhorsed or wounded. Lucan himself suffered a minor wound and his horse was hit twice. Yet on he went towards No. 3 redoubt. Looking back

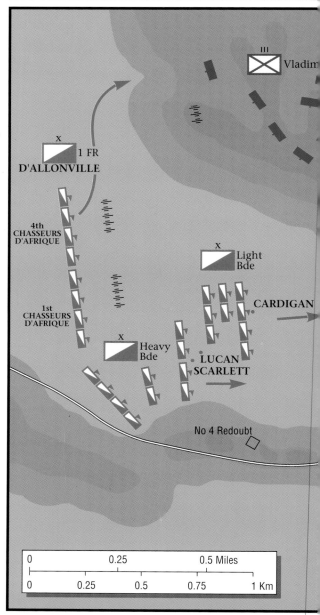

Charge of the Light Briga

there, he realized that the Heavy Brigade was struggling under concentrated cross-fire from Russian infantry and batteries now fully alive to the serious nature of the events unfolding before them. If both brigades had been together, there would have been sense in riding on. To continue, Lucan reasoned, would be to risk sacrificing both. Better to halt the Heavy Brigade. It could then

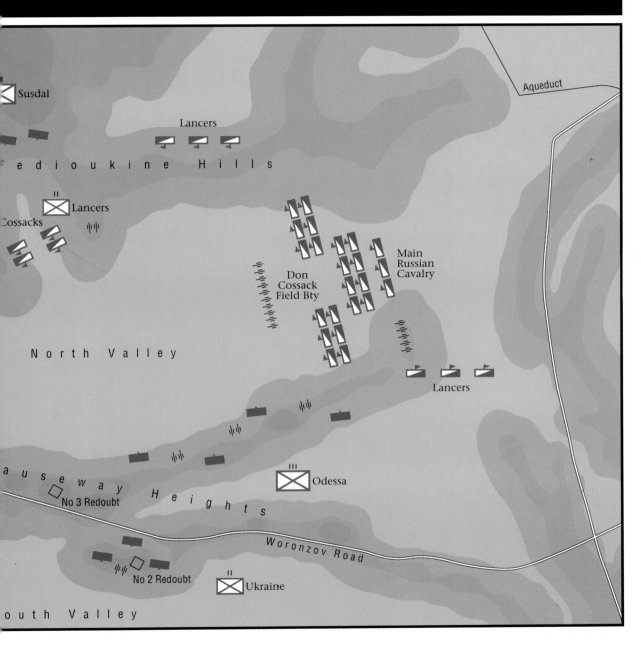

cover the Light Brigade as it returned down the Valley. Remarking to his wounded ADC, Lord William Paulet, 'They have sacrificed the Light Brigade: they shall not the Heavy, if I can help it', he ordered Scarlett to halt and retire his men back out of range of the hostile fire. It was a wise decision. The Royals alone already had 21 killed or disabled (with wounds to themselves or their horses), their commanding officer (Lieutenant-Colonel John Yorke) having sustained a badly shattered leg, three other officers being seriously wounded and another having had his horse shot from under him.

When the Heavy Brigade pulled back, Cardigan was already running the gauntlet of shot, shell and grape from three sides. During the early

▼ *Charge of the Light Brigade. Although the artist does show riderless horses and wounded men, the lines are altogether too regular and the formation is, in fact, not accurate. There were two regiments (four squadrons) in the first line, but only one in the second (11th Hussars). The two regiments in the third line had by this stage separated, with Shewell's 8th Hussars dropping behind to the right. The overall impression, however, showing the weight of Russian infantry and artillery fire is reasonable. The redoubts are in the middle distance, Balaclava in the centre background. (Sandhurst)*

stages of the advance, enemy fire was not concentrated; moreover, Cardigan kept a strict hold over the following troops. When, as he later admitted, Captain White of the 17th Lancers tried to 'force the pace . . . anxious to get out of the murderous fire and into the guns', he came level with his brigade commander, Cardigan's gesture of reproof was to lay his sword across White's chest. Obediently, White fell back.

Gaps were beginning to appear as saddles were emptied and horses fell screaming and writhing. Constant orders to 'close up' files came hoarsely through the gathering smoke. A hundred yards from the Don Battery, Maxse was wounded, and

Wombwell had his horse killed beneath him. With no staff in attendance, Cardigan rode on in splendid isolation, statuesque, sword still at the slope. Eighty yards to go, and a crashing salvo erupted from the enemy battery. It was almost at point-blank range. The first line seemed to disintegrate. Oldham of the 13th Dragoons went down, and the 17th Lancers lost several officers in this terrible discharge. More gaps appeared in the ranks. As it reached the guns, the first line numbered scarcely more than 50 out of the 270 who had set out.

And behind it, the other three regiments lost their order even before feeling the full weight of the enemy fire. Douglas's 11th Hussars kept well up on the left. The third line, however, became divided. Aware of Cardigan's last instruction, 'I expect your best support; mind, Sir George, your best support!', Paget pressed the 4th Light Dragoons forward, tending to follow the 13th Light Dragoons, while Douglas supported Morris's 17th Lancers. On Paget's right, therefore, the 8th Hussars instinctively veered more towards the Causeway Heights; and the distance between the two third-line regiments increased as Shewell elected to keep a steady pace throughout. By the time that they reached No. 3 redoubt, therefore, these three regiments were echeloned back from the left: 11th Hussars, 4th Light Dragoons, 8th Hussars. Their progress was further threatened by the increasing intensity of enemy fire and the groaning, bleeding men and horses ahead of them, which must be avoided. Riderless mounts were beginning to discomfort them too. Several plunged back westwards, while others turned to join the charge. At one point, Paget was flanked on each side by four or five such horses.

Cardigan, travelling by his own estimate at 17mph, was only ten yards from the Don Battery when the destructive last salvo was fired. Miraculously unharmed, he rode safely between two artillery pieces. Behind him some 17th Lancers fought the enemy gunners, many of whom resisted bravely as others cowered beneath their weapons. Morris led twenty of the Regiment around the battery to the left. Clearing the smoke, this small band saw literally hundreds of grey-coated

Russian cavalry before them – just standing. Without hesitation, Morris charged, running through the nearest officer, as his tiny force drove wildly into the ranks. Astonishingly, the enemy wavered and his centre gave way. Soon, however, some rallied together with Cossacks from the flanks. Morris's men were in grave peril.

So was Morris himself. Unable to free his sword from the dead officer, he was effectively tethered to the ground by the transfixed corpse,

▲*Charge of the Light Brigade: a scene at the Don Battery. Note the Russians with fixed* *bayonets and the soldier with the thick greatcoat in the centre. (Warner)*

and was struck two hefty blows on the head. He fell unconscious. Coming round, Morris found his sword mysteriously free but Cossacks with sharp lances surrounding him. Whirling his sword in a circle, he kept the lances at bay while sustaining another deep wound. Then a Russian officer came to his rescue and accepted his sword in surrender. He was indeed lucky. Elsewhere, marauding Cossacks were busy finishing off the wounded, although several unhorsed cavalrymen were made prisoner.

Cardigan was not one of them. Emerging through the guns, their attendant limbers and tumbrils, he too came face to face with a large body of cavalry. Eagerly the Cossacks eyed his finery. But Prince Radzvill, their commander, recognized

◄ Lieutenant-Colonel Lord George Paget. Commanding officer of the 4th (The Queen's Own) Regiment of Dragoons, part of the Light Brigade in the Crimea. Paget rode across the South Valley with Lord Lucan on his dawn reconnaissance on 25 October 1854. He was therefore a witness to the opening exchanges of the Battle of Balaclava. Briefly in charge of the Brigade until Lord Cardigan arrived after spending the night in his yacht in Balaclava harbour, Paget commanded the third line of the charge and rallied survivors of his regiment beyond the Russian field battery at the end of the Valley. Just before the order to advance was given, Paget lit a cigar which he continued to smoke during the action. He was one of the last to return up the Valley from the Charge of the Light Brigade. (Selby)

Cardigan from social events that he had attended when living in England. He offered a reward if the Light Brigade commander were taken alive. Ten Cossacks therefore circled Cardigan, pushing their lances edgily towards him. Contemptuously, with his sword even now at the slope, Cardigan turned round and rode through their ineffective screen. Down the Valley he went again, his duty done. He had led the Brigade to its objective. Riding back, he looked neither to right nor left. Reaching Scarlett, his first reaction was to complain about Nolan's ill-discipline. Amid all that carnage and loss, this remained uppermost in his mind. The Heavy Brigade commander cut him short, telling him that he had just ridden over Nolan's body. At that, Cardigan resumed his course towards the Sapoune Ridge. Over a mile to the east, the remnants of his regiments were still fighting for their lives.

Surviving the Charge

The Brigade Major (George Mayow) had gathered fifteen 17th Lancers from around the guns and, like Morris, advanced eastwards, to find himself confronted by the many Russian reserves within sight of the aqueduct close to the Tchernaya crossing. Away to his left, after Morris's capture, his remaining men were met by Sergeant O'Hara, who led them back down the Valley, skirting Cossacks advancing from the right flank. Beyond the Don Battery, Captain Soame Jenyns rallied a small group of 13th Dragoons.

So much for the first line. What of the following three regiments at the guns? The 11th Hussars overlapped the Russian field battery on the left, though the right squadron passed through the guns, now silent. Halting past the limbers, Douglas saw complete confusion. One Russian officer surrendered his sword, without resistance, to a subaltern. As the 11th went forward again, Douglas too came upon the Russian reserves. He was now hopelessly outnumbered. Without hesitation, however, he reformed and charged. Not for the first, nor last, time that day, the superior enemy force gave way – to be pursued by the 11th into the gorge leading to the Tchernaya.

About thirty yards behind Douglas, Paget led the 4th Dragoons through the swirling gloom to see enemy mounted gunners about to tow away the guns. Responding to a strident 'tally ho!' from one officer, the regiment hacked its way into and through the battery. Those not free to use their sabres fired pistols. The 4th, once it resumed its advance, was now a long way behind Douglas. Away to the right, the 8th Hussars had lost about half its strength before reaching the battery. But it did so in good order, and trotted on some 300 yards beyond. Here Shewell halted to consider the position. After pausing for about five minutes, he continued to advance to come up unexpectedly with Mayow and his fifteen 17th Lancers, who joined forces with him.

At this stage of the battle, a little over 200 men were in the general area of the enemy position at the far end of the North Valley, though not all were organized into groups. For the most part, they were actually confronting Russians, though some of the British were far in advance of others as they chased the grey greatcoats towards the Techernaya. In the centre, no discernible formation existed. However, in advance on the left, Douglas had about fifty men of the 11th; to his right rear, Paget also mustered some fifty 4th Dragoons. On the far right, Shewell had about seventy, including the small body of 17th Lancers under Mayow. Each of these formations was acting independently.

Looking back down the Valley, Shewell realized that the Russian infantry, drawn up in squares on the Causeway Heights were still untouched and that, more critically, enemy lancers were debouching from the same area to bar his way back. Sensing extreme danger, Shewell ordered: 'Right about wheel!' And for the first time that day, he exceeded a trot. His 70 charged the 300 lancers manoeuvring behind them. Waiting for their third squadron to get into line, the Russians received Shewell's charge while stationary, and the 8th crashed through, suffering very few casualties. The shock of Shewell's charge scattered the Russians towards both sides of the Valley. Through the gap thus created, Jenyns led his tiny cluster of 13th Dragoons. They and Shewell still had to endure fire from the Causeway Heights. But, as with the first-line survivors that picked their way ahead of them, they were spared crossfire from the Fedioukine Hills.

For this they had French cavalry to thank. Riding down from the Chersonese Uplands, the commander of the French Cavalry Division (General Morris) reached the two regiments of *Chasseurs d'Afrique* which formed his 1st Brigade under d'Allonville. Watching Cardigan, Lucan and Scarlett set off down the North Valley, Morris dispatched d'Allonville with the 4th Regiment to attack the Russian forces on the Fedioukine Hills, where two half-batteries (each of four guns) were guarded by two infantry battalions and two squadrons of Cossacks. Charging up the slope through scrubland and tall undergrowth, the French put the enemy to flight with scant trouble. When Zhaboritski in person led the Vladimir Regiment in an attempt to cut off the French retreat, d'Allonville reacted swiftly to withdraw his men from danger. The *Chasseurs d'Afrique* lost 10 killed and 28 wounded, but they ensured that on its way back down the Valley no cannon from the Fedioukine Hills would sweep the Light Brigade.

At the other end of the Valley, the 11th Hussars, accepting that further progress against the large enemy body near the aqueduct was impossible, began to make its way back. Seeing their enemy turn away, the Russians took heart, and soon the 11th found themselves being chased. Joined by Paget and survivors of the 4th Dragoons, they saw their pursuers gaining rapidly on them. As the senior officer, Paget took charge of the

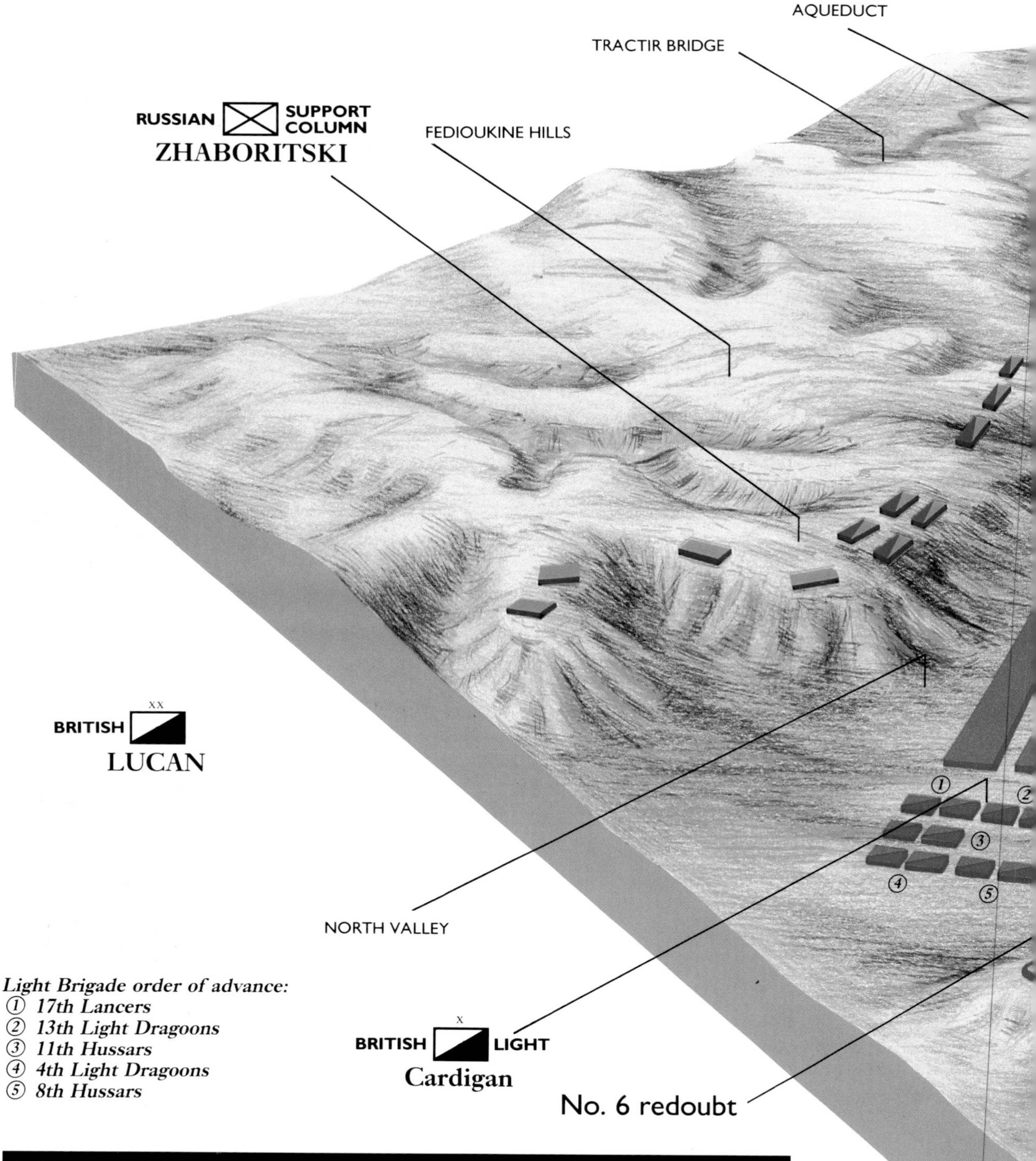
AQUEDUCT
TRACTIR BRIDGE
RUSSIAN SUPPORT COLUMN
ZHABORITSKI
FEDIOUKINE HILLS
BRITISH
XX
LUCAN
NORTH VALLEY
Light Brigade order of advance:
① 17th Lancers
② 13th Light Dragoons
③ 11th Hussars
④ 4th Light Dragoons
⑤ 8th Hussars
BRITISH LIGHT
X
Cardigan
No. 6 redoubt
①
②
③
④
⑤

THE CHARGE OF THE LIGHT BRIGADE

11.00 to 11.20am, 25 October 1854: Phase 3 of the Battle of Balaclava

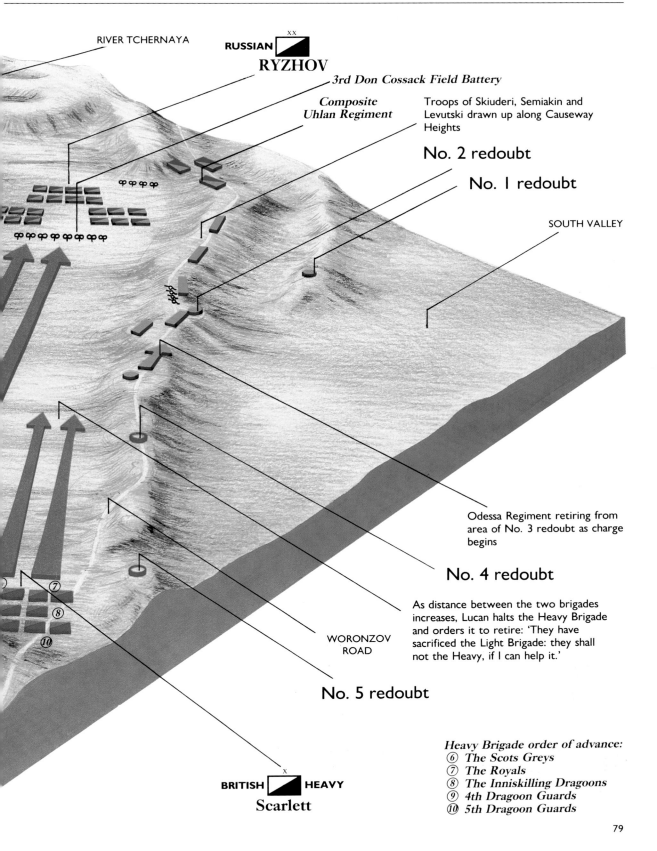

RIVER TCHERNAYA

RUSSIAN ᵡᵡ

RYZHOV

3rd Don Cossack Field Battery

Composite Uhlan Regiment

Troops of Skiuderi, Semiakin and Levutski drawn up along Causeway Heights

No. 2 redoubt

No. 1 redoubt

SOUTH VALLEY

Odessa Regiment retiring from area of No. 3 redoubt as charge begins

No. 4 redoubt

As distance between the two brigades increases, Lucan halts the Heavy Brigade and orders it to retire: 'They have sacrificed the Light Brigade: they shall not the Heavy, if I can help it.'

WORONZOV ROAD

No. 5 redoubt

BRITISH ˣ **HEAVY**

Scarlett

Heavy Brigade order of advance:
⑥ *The Scots Greys*
⑦ *The Royals*
⑧ *The Inniskilling Dragoons*
⑨ *4th Dragoon Guards*
⑩ *5th Dragoon Guards*

combined force. He realized that if their retreat continued they would be overwhelmed. To the surviving 70 men with him, he therefore called: 'If you don't front, my boys, we are done!' By turning round again, the 11th Hussars and 4th Dragoons shocked the Russians. Bewildered, they came to a halt. For a few minutes both forces looked blankly at one another. Then Lieutenant Palmer of the 11th Hussars glanced westwards down the Valley to see a large body of lancers forming up across their line of retreat. Momentarily, Douglas mistook them for British troops, but was quickly corrected. Between two powerful bodies of Russian cavalry – to the front and rear – they might yet be done for. 'What the devil shall we do?', Paget mused aloud. Quickly he decided: 'Threes about.' They would fight their way out. With their numbers swelled by stragglers, the remnants of the two regiments faced about, assumed a rough formation (with no time to dress properly) and prepared to break through the enemy lancers.

This time, the Russians did not make the mistake of being unprepared. Unlike Shewell, Paget would not escape that way. Drawing up his four squadrons in twos, the Russian commander half-wheeled them back to allow him opportunity for a flank attack. He then began to advance against the British line of retreat, but for some strange reason repeated the Russian failure so often seen on 25 October: he stopped. The right of the Russian formation had edged ahead so that the whole line was at an oblique angle to the British squadrons. In practice, only this right extension caused even minor trouble, as the British used their swords successfully to fend off tentative prods. One officer later wrote: 'There is one explanation, and one only – the hand of God was upon us!'

In fact, Russian gunners also contrived to cover the retreating regiments in a strange way. They continued to fire, which discouraged any Russian cavalry pursuit, as the escaping horsemen laboured uphill towards the Sapoune Ridge. En route, they rode over the pathetic remains of many of their fellows less fortunate that day. Paget's horse slowed badly, and the 4th Dragoons' commanding officer was one of the last to reach safety. Seeing his brigade commander dismounted, he said:

'Holloa! Lord Cardigan, were you not there?' 'Wasn't I, though', replied Cardigan. 'Here, Jenyns, did not you see me at the guns?' Jenyns agreed. This light-hearted exchange was no more than a greeting between men who knew that they had fought hard. Later, it would be maliciously used to infer that Cardigan had not taken part in the charge.

The cameo scene between Cardigan, Paget and Jenyns was only one remarkable episode during that brief, searing period in the North Valley. Lieutenant Wombwell, Cardigan's ADC who had been unseated close to the Don Battery, mounted a stray only to have that horse shot from under him as well. Surrounded by Cossacks and disarmed, he became a prisoner. With his badly slashed head bleeding profusely, his captors brought Morris to join Wombwell. Scarcely had Morris arrived, than Wombwell saw another loose horse, dashed through the ring of enemy lancers to mount and gallop away to come up with Paget's retiring 4th Dragoons.

This left Morris stranded and, moreover, his protective officer soon rode off, whereupon the Cossacks began to rob him. Although by now weak from loss of blood, like Wombwell he managed to break away and take refuge in the smoke and confusion. He, too, caught a stray, but fell off – unconscious. Coming round, he realized that a hovering Cossack was about to run him through. With the energy of a terror-stricken man, Morris heaved himself up and took to his heels. Once more the smoke and dust saved him and, fortuitously, another stray appeared at hand. After a short ride, this horse was killed and, once more, Morris lost consciousness. Recovering his senses, he found the dead animal lying across his legs, trapping him. With a supreme effort, considering his physical state and all that he had been through during and since the charge, he managed to wriggle free and stumble away up the Valley. Almost level with No. 4 redoubt he came across Nolan's body. The shock of the discovery – the corpse of his close friend – combined with three severe head wounds, a fractured right arm and several fractured ribs not unreasonably made him faint again. When he came round this time, he was safe in a British tent.

Lieutenant Clowes was not so fortunate. Wounded by grape-shot and unhorsed, he survived the unwelcome attention of ravaging Cos-

▼ *Another scene at the Don Battery. This time, the Russians are fighting* back, but the gun in the centre has been overturned. (Warner)

sacks, who were busy unceremoniously dispatching many of the wounded around him. But he was too weak to catch and mount a loose horse. Once the smoke cleared, he was seen and taken prisoner. Lieutenant Phillips was luckier. Having lost his horse, he was busily defending himself and a

trooper who had been disabled in both hands, when a trumpet recalled their Cossack tormentors. Officer and trooper managed then to reach safety at a painful shuffle. Another trooper, also, owed his life to a caring officer. Several of the Light Brigade, riding back, saw Major de Salis of the 8th Hussars leading his horse westwards with a wounded cavalryman lolling in the saddle. They deserved to survive; and they did.

When the residue of the Light Brigade was drawn up on the slopes of the South Valley, appropriately looking towards Balaclava, Cardigan addressed it with feeling. 'Men! It is a mad-brained trick, but it is no fault of mine.' 'Never mind, my lord', answered a voice from the ranks, 'we are ready to go again.' Perhaps. But the cost of the exercise had been dire. Of the 673 men who went into action, the Light Brigade could muster only 195; 113 men had been killed, 247 badly wounded; 475 horses had been lost, and a further 42 injured. Only two officers of the first line and the accompanying brigade staff emerged from the slaughter unscathed. Cardigan was himself wounded; and his bravery was never in serious doubt. Morris, leading the 17th Lancers, just behind him, declared: 'Nothing could be better. He put himself just where he ought, about in front of my right squadron, and went down in capital style.'

At 11.20, the fourth and last phase of the Battle of Balaclava was effectively over, although occasional artillery duels continued into the afternoon. Neither the Duke of Cambridge nor Sir George Cathcart were able to influence its outcome with their divisions. Cambridge, in association with one of the French infantry brigades deployed on the Plain near the Col, did clear the remaining Russians off the Fedioukine Hills; and Cathcart exchanged fire with infantry on the Causeway Heights. But the real battle had already ended.

Overlooking the battlefield from the Sapoune Ridge, the French general Bosquet observing the Light Brigade's desperate charge uttered words that have become a celebrated epitaph: 'C'est magnifique, mais ce n'est pas la guerre.' A Russian commentator reached much the same conclusion: 'It is difficult to do justice to the feat of these mad cavalry.'

▼*Embarkation of Sick. Here sick and wounded soldiers are being ferried to ships in Balaclava Harbour. This route to hospitals across the Black Sea would have been lost, with disastrous effects for the movement of* *casualties let alone the implications for the supply line to the Chersonese Uplands, if the Russians had succeeded in cutting off the port on 25 October 1854. (Sandhurst)*

AFTERMATH: COUNTING THE COST

Scarcely had the last trooper limped back to the shelter of the Sapoune Ridge than the recriminations began. Who was responsible for the plight of the Light Brigade? Its crippling loss of 475 horses alone had removed its effectiveness as a fighting force.

Riding down to the Plain, Raglan angrily rebuked Cardigan: 'What do you mean, sir, by attacking a battery in front, contrary to all the usages of warfare, and the customs of the service?' To which the commander of the Light Brigade replied stiffly: 'My lord, I hope you will not blame me, for I received the order to attack from my superior officer in front of the troops.' Nor did Lucan escape the commander-in-chief's censure: 'You have lost the Light Brigade!', he bitingly exclaimed, going on to stress that his order had been to advance on the 'Heights' and to recover 'our lost English guns'.

The dispute as to what precisely passed verbally between individuals (principally Lucan, Cardigan and Nolan) and who was therefore chiefly responsible for the Light Brigade débâcle rumbled on quite literally for years. It involved cross-accusations, statements in Parliament and the law courts. It is difficult, however vague Raglan's fourth order may seem, to justify launching cavalry downhill along the North Valley, when Lucan was ordered to advance on 'heights' (as Raglan afterwards pointed out). Furthermore, there was no indication that the Russians had begun to tow away the Don Battery guns before

▼ *Scutari Hospital, end of the casualty route across the Black Sea from Balaclava. A ward in one of the hospitals at Scutari, where 'The Lady with the Lamp' (Florence Nightingale) made such an impression. (Sandhurst)*

◀Balaclava Harbour. This shows the port in 1855, once the wharves had been improved. Note the light railway running along the quay. This carried supplies up to the troops before Sevastopol, having been constructed by civilian contractors. (Sandhurst)

Below: Outside Balaclava Harbour. On 14 November a hurricane swept the Allied camps. Many ships caught outside Balaclava harbour foundered, underlining its worth as a sheltered anchorage. (Sandhurst)

the attack. What Nolan and Lucan said to one another therefore becomes critical. The ADC must have been fully aware of Lord Raglan's requirements: earlier in the day another ADC (Captain Wetherall) had interpreted a previous order to withdraw Lucan's division along the South Valley after loss of the Turkish redoubts.

Thus the personalities of the men concerned do become extremely important. Cardigan and Lucan detested one another, so their relationship remained cool, formal and professional. No room for rational discussion here. Nolan, an excitable half-Italian contemptuous of Lucan's failure for over half an hour to execute Lord Raglan's third order, was not the best person calmly to explain the commander-in-chief's intention. Whether Nolan's later extraordinary dash to the fore constituted a desperate attempt to point the Light Brigade towards its true objective remains unclear. His death neatly removed any possibility of later cross-examination.

Who Won?

Whatever the reasons for carrying out the charge, the Russians were given a first-class opportunity to claim victory on 25 October through its perceived failure. Events on the ground can always be turned to maximum advantage by commanders in skilfully compiled dispatches. Liprandi proved no exception in this respect. He claimed to have taken eight guns in the three captured redoubts plus four destroyed (in No. 4). He further explained that Cardigan had led 2,000 cavalry down the North Valley, losing 400 dead, 60 seriously wounded and 22 prisoners (the actual figures being respectively, 113, 247 and 15). The engagements involving Campbell at Kadikoi and

Scarlett's Heavy Brigade were not mentioned. In turn, Menshikov reported to the Tsar that Cardigan had attacked the hussar brigade of the 6th Cavalry Division and been decimated by the flank attack of four squadrons of the Composite Uhlan Regiment together with cross-fire from riflemen and artillery of the 12th and 16th Infantry Divisions. Menshikov claimed that eleven, not eight, guns had been taken, and that his own losses in dead and wounded were under 300 (in fact, 238 were killed and 312 badly wounded).

The claims of Liprandi and Menshikov may have been exaggerated but, in truth, the Russians had good reason to be satisfied with the day. They had mounted a successful attack on the redoubts, and they had tangible evidence of their triumph in the captured guns and a Turkish standard taken from No. 1 redoubt. Liprandi was certainly in control of the eastern part of the Causeway Heights, which he reinforced with more troops during the afternoon of 25 October. Although he would voluntarily withdraw from there and all land west of the Tchernaya within six weeks, for the moment he had gained distinct territorial advantage. He had quite obviously broken the outer defences of Balaclava. Destruction of the Light Brigade (which, whatever damage it had wrought to the Don Battery, had itself captured no guns) was also clear.

On the other hand, the British had cause for satisfaction as well. The personal bravery of the troops involved – including any dispassionate assessment of the Turks in No. 1 redoubt, who held out against vastly superior odds for 1½ hours – cannot be disputed. Moreover, two very important actions had been won. The hypercritical might note that Campbell, even without the two Turkish battalions, had a numerical advantage of almost 2:1 over the attacking Russian squadrons at Kadikoi. His troops were, also, behind cover in defensive positions against which any cavalry (and light cavalry in particular) were professionally loath to ride. Yet, had Kadikoi fallen, the gorge to Balaclava and the vulnerable British supply line would have been open for later, if not immediate, attack. Liprandi could have advanced his infantry across the South Valley almost at will. Lord Raglan would then, as he feared, have been required to choose

between that threat to his supply line or the siege. 'The Thin Red Line', if on examination perhaps not quite so thin, was nevertheless vital to the survival of troops on the Chersonese Uplands.

Scarlett's achievement does not deserve to be overshadowed by the more spectacular series of events ninety minutes later in the North Valley. Had the Heavy Brigade not put 2,000 Russians to flight, at a cost of a mere 78 British casualties, Campbell would have faced a much more potent assault than one of 400 tentative horsemen. Scarlett and Campbell thus deserve more credit in the broad picture of the battle than posterity often ascribes to them.

To some extent, the Battle of Balaclava in its four distinct phases – redoubts, Kadikoi, Heavy and Light Brigade actions – may be seen as a draw. Russian occupation of the Causeway Heights had a marginal effect on the British supply lines via Kadikoi and the Col. Only a small amount of equipment had been moved across the South Valley and along the Woronzov Road – a route now perilously within range of Russian troops. The Russians could justifiably claim material victory at the redoubts and in the North Valley;

▲Balaclava. The second winter, when Sevastopol south of the Bay had fallen into Allied hands. Note how the railway has been developed. But the harbour is clearly still crowded. Without its successful defence on 25 October 1854 none of this, which eased the passage of supplies to the troops, would have been possible. (Sandhurst)

▶Top: Grim scene at Balaclava, as the supply columns wend their way away from the wharves up to the Chersonese Uplands during the second winter of the war, a grim reminder of the cost in human lives of the conflict. Note, too, the line of graves on the left. (Sandhurst)

▶Supply Route. Huts and warm clothing being transported from Balaclava towards Kadikoi. (Sandhurst)

but, conversely, the British prevailed through Campbell and Scarlett. The moral ascendancy achieved by the British over the Russian cavalry was stark. The curious, but consistent, reluctance of its squadrons seriously to tangle with the British as the day wore on was marked. And the battle had also shown the value and effectiveness of inter-Allied cooperation, which d'Allonville's clearance of the Fedioukine Hills had aptly demonstrated.